TESTIMONIES

TESTIMONIES

lesbian and bisexual coming-out stories

Edited by Sarah Holmes and Jenn Tust

alyson books
los angeles | new york

© 1988, 1994, 2002 BY ALYSON PUBLICATIONS. ALL RIGHTS RESERVED.
AUTHORS RETAIN COPYRIGHT TO THEIR INDIVIDUAL PIECES OF WORK.

MANUFACTURED IN THE UNITED STATES OF AMERICA.

THIS TRADE PAPERBACK ORIGINAL IS PUBLISHED BY ALYSON PUBLICATIONS,
P.O. BOX 4371, LOS ANGELES, CALIFORNIA 90078-4371.
DISTRIBUTION IN THE UNITED KINGDOM BY
TURNAROUND PUBLISHER SERVICES LTD.,
UNIT 3, OLYMPIA TRADING ESTATE, COBURG ROAD, WOOD GREEN,
LONDON N22 6TZ ENGLAND.

FIRST EDITION: OCTOBER 1988
SECOND EDITION: JANUARY 1994
THIRD EDITION: AUGUST 2002

02 03 04 05 06 **a** 10 9 8 7 6 5 4 3 2 1

ISBN 1-55583-546-5

LIBRARY OF CONGRESS CATALOGING-IN-PUBLICATION DATA
   TESTIMONIES : LESBIAN COMING-OUT STORIES.—3RD ED. / EDITED BY
   SARAH HOLMES AND JENN TUST.
      ISBN 1-55583-546-5
      1. LESBIANS—UNITED STATES—PSYCHOLOGY. 2. LESBIANS—UNITED
   STATES—IDENTITY. 3. LESBIANS—UNITED STATES—SEXUAL BEHAVIOR.
   4. COMING OUT (SEXUAL ORIENTATION)—UNITED STATES. I. HOLMES,
   SARAH. II. TUST, JENN.
   HQ75.5.T49 2002
   305.48'9664—DC21   2002070900

CREDITS
- ELLEN S. JAFFE'S "DREAM-CATCHER" APPEARED IN *INTRICATE COUN-
  TRIES: WOMEN POETS FROM EARTH TO SKY*, EDITED BY GERTRUDE
  LEBANS (ARTEMIS ENTERPRISES, 1996).
- COVER DESIGN BY MATT SAMS.
- COVER PHOTOGRAPHY BY PHOTODISC.

CONTENTS

Introduction

Why write or read coming-out stories? Lesbians, gay men, and bisexual people have always told stories of their relationships, as other people do, yet coming out has a potency and meaning for us that is subtly different. Whether you are lesbian, bisexual, gay, or transgendered, or simply reading about their lives, the selections in this book offer a wide, varied, and moving look at lesbian and bisexual women's experiences.

Coming out occurs when a person first acknowledges feelings of attraction and/or strong affection for a person, or people, of the same gender, and decides that they are lesbian, bisexual, or gay. It is a continual process; it takes place throughout people's lives whenever someone discusses or acknowledges their sexual or affectional preference for a person of the same gender.

Coming-out stories and poems have long been a part of lesbian and bisexual lore. Whether written in journals and letters, revealed in paintings or photos, told socially, recounted at public events such as readings or poetry slams, or published in anthologies such as this one, coming-out stories tell of women's intimate, passionate, and sexual relationships with other women—in the same way that straight people commemorate their partnerships with wedding announcements and photographs. Lesbian and bisexual relationships, social networks, and political associations are much like everyone else's; a woman may have a partner of the same gender, but in many ways people are still just people. Lesbian and bisexual women date, fall in and out of love, stay in love and marry, raise children, and sometimes divorce or break up. Friendships may continue throughout one's life; other friendships come and go. They are often part of families that are as diverse as families can be, and they are increasingly open about our sexual orientations at work. Sexual orientation may change over time for some people. For others it is, and always has been, the same.

Social and political trends have come, gone, and sometimes stayed in lesbian and bisexual communities—commitment ceremonies, same-sex marriages, political correctness, polyamory, consciousness-raising groups, live chat, collectives, Gen-X sex radicalism, the lesbian baby boom, second-generation feminist conservatives, and queer identity politics, for example. Same-gender relationships have always been a part of cultures, and these relations have often been intimate and sexual. The way these intimacies have transpired and been described has varied a great deal according to the era and the culture. Often they have been discouraged and repressed, yet they have also been a recognized and valued part of people's lives, desires, imaginations, and economic and political systems. *Testimonies* features writings by contemporary American, Australian, British, Canadian, Filipino, and Zimbabwean women that offer a glimpse into women's lives throughout the world during recent decades.

The women who have contributed to this anthology have come to their orientations at different points in their lives. Therefore we have grouped the stories into five sections: "The Early Years," "On Our Own," "Best Friends," "Married and Later," and "Snapshots." Some of these stories were published in the first and/or second editions of *Testimonies* (Alyson Publications, 1988 and 1994). We are pleased to include these vital stories alongside many new, rich, and inspiring contributions.

As issues regarding sexual orientation, gender, intimacy,

and morality continue to shift as we move further into the 21st century, all of these stories offer insight into the compelling power and rewarding intimacies of lesbian and bisexual women. We hope you enjoy your reading.

—Sarah Holmes

The Early Years

Home

Nona Caspers

For me there was no one clinching moment, mad love, or political leap that landed me in Lesbos. Coming out to myself and to others was a matter of finding a way to survive and letting myself thrive.

I was one of those wispy white-haired girls, born into rural Minnesota, Catholicism, and the '60s. My strong legs were wrapped in itchy pink tights and hidden under synthetic frills. I remember twirling round and round in the driveway, with my long hair flying, and skirts flapping like feminine flags. I was happy. I had a neighborhood full of Catholic girlfriends. We played SPUD, Annie Annie Over, Wonder Bread Communion, Chinese Sticks, dolls, and another game we called Tickle. We would climb, four at a time, one on each pole of a swingset, mishmashing our vulvas against the metal until a tickle rooted between our legs and sprouted throughout our blessed bodies. We giggled and talked to one another the whole time. Vicky, Beth, or Lisa's face hung across from mine. It was an intimate, soothing, and sacred girl ritual.

Then there was Romeo and Juliet—we took turns being one or the other. We held hands and kissed, passionately twisting our lips together like Steve and Rachel on *Another World*. I remember the times we slept at one another's houses and cuddled up close like two chips melting together. And we'd talk: intense, excited talk that mixed our thoughts and feelings together like dough.

I felt safe and warm during those years. The closeness, these friendships were what life was all about. Nobody said

3

anything to me about the touching. We were just little girls playing.

By the seventh grade, with breasts and blood approaching, my childhood safety had disappeared. In my rural high school, the "sexual revolution" meant girls felt more pressure, called "freedom," to revolve around the penis. While the Church encouraged my "safe" friendships with girls, the coolest, bravest deed was to touch a boy. I started to hang out with the most heterosexually active girls. We would sit nose to nose, knee to knee, whispering, with my long hair floating between our intense faces. Our words and voices mingled, rose and fell. Our closeness depended on telling every detail; I had nothing to tell. Certain boys made me nervous and took these feelings to be crushes. But I preferred being with my girlfriends talking about it than with those boys, doing something about it—and for all their boy-crazy activity, they did too.

As the pressure increased, I became extremely anxious. I began to sense that there was something wrong with me. Not the usual zit on the tip of my nose or "Tell me the truth, am I weird?" insecurities of adolescence. I felt a cold, white secret, a longing, lodged beneath my rib cage. I had to guard this spot from everyone, even myself. I acted like a tough femme—seductive, confident. I entertained my girlfriends by getting into trouble: sassing at teachers, running loud, wild, and bold. I remember sneaking apples from a yard we passed during our daily Phys. Ed. run and giving them to my newest close friend, Carrie. Teachers kicked me out of classes and told me to "act like a lady." Although my girlfriends admired my guts, I felt scared every minute of every day, as though at any time some filth would spill out of me, rolling and clanging on the streets for everyone to see. The only part I could name was the fear.

I became preoccupied with trying to figure out how I would ever be in a heterosexual relationship, as there seemed to be no other kind. The intimacy and emotional attachments with girlfriends and, later, women friends, came so easily and felt so natural and fulfilling. Intimacy with men felt so impossible, so utterly out of reach and dangerous. Yet, in the world I grew up in, heterosexuality was inevitable. The only women I had ever know that got out of it were nuns. I did *not* want to be a nun.

I remember two isolated and very buried incidents in my teen years, when my emotional attractions became sexualized. Carrie invited me over to her house, seven miles from my hometown of Melrose, Minnesota. I remember being very excited. I dressed carefully, brushed my long, blond hair until the brush bristles sagged, and accentuated my breasts. I thought of her breasts, how they had popped out and were so fleshy and firm. A hope dug its way to the surface of my thoughts, with a vague wish that something might happen and Carrie might want to play.

We were sitting in her older sister's car, going through her purse, when we found a flat round pillbox with the days of the week printed on it. Carrie asked me if I know what they were. I did. We sat quiet a long time, and the air thickened. Then she asked me if I wanted to play a boy-girl game. I acted dumb and said, "Sure," praying to the Catholic God I'd grown up with that she meant what I thought. She did. I remember clearly how our bodies folded so comfortably together. I felt warm and safe—like home. I thought it couldn't last. It could only be practice for the real thing. We were just playing.

The next time we were sexual was two years later. As she invited me, she said that she knew two boys, Kenny and Bob, who would meet us at a café. I was anxious and felt sick, but I wanted to be with her, to talk and talk and laugh into the night. My stomach pains went away when the boys didn't show up and we returned to her house. Finally, we lay in bed and I pretended to be asleep. My skin tingled as I wished that she would touch me. She did. I stayed half asleep, not daring to respond as she moved my hands over her breasts. I mumbled "Kenny"; she whispered "Bob." In the morning we could not look each other in the eye. We both said, "I had a dream about a boy."

Soon after this dream, I made a few drugged, drunken attempts to connect with the other gender. Boys liked me, but I didn't seem to care about them. I retreated into starvation and obsessive exercise. I whittled away my female flesh, my anger, my fears, my sexuality. My goal in life was to be able to wear my 12-year-old brother's Levi's. I did. I was 16.

When I was 21, I was hiding two things—my eating patterns and my virginity. At times, I lied. I had avoided contact with men as much as possible, continuing to seek out close women friends wherever I went. But enough was enough, I finally told myself. If I could hike alone through Guatemala, climb volcanoes, live in a tepee and out of a van, put up 11 cords of wood, and get A's in chemistry, then surely I could develop a "normal" emotional and sexual relationship with a nice man.

I picked Doc. We were both planting trees in the South. He turned out to be gay, or "bisexual with a heavy emotional inclination toward men." After our first bout of intercourse, he asked me if I was a lesbian. I laughed and said no with confidence.

Lesbians were somebody else. Lesbians were the women in the lesbian section of *Our Bodies, Our Selves*—women with short hair and caps, standing together with arms across shoulders, hands cupping each other's breasts—those were lesbians. The scenes in *Going Down With Janice*, Peggy Caserta's unscrupulous book, which I read secretly in high school—that was lesbianism. Kim, a girl in high school who carved her name into her arm and gifted me with stolen incense burners before she ran off the California, and then called me up and told me she had a wife—she was a lesbian. A lesbian was a woman who had sex with women, who craved sex with women, who creamed her jeans whenever she was with women—I didn't, I wasn't. I creamed my jeans for no one.

Ironically, I held some admiration, awe, and respect for lesbians. As an ex-Catholic, I held on to the feeling that somehow it was better to fool around with women than to be defiled by men. Being lesbian was close to being a nun. Lesbians were different; sometimes, they looked comfortable, playful, happy, and independent. At other times, I saw them as fad-hoppers, immature, and ill. Mostly, I didn't think of them at all, and neither did anyone else I knew.

Right Back Where I Started From

Karen X. Tulchinsky

When I was a child, I thought I was going to grow up and marry a woman. I believed it with all my heart and soul. At bedtime, when my mother would read fairy tales to me and my sister, I'd imagine myself as the prince, perched handsomely on top of a majestic horse, riding from town to town, searching for my one true princess. I was the "knight in shining armor" who went off into the countryside to slay dragons and bring back their heads for my queen. When I played house with my best friend, Brenda, I was the father and she was the mother. I was the doctor, she was the nurse.

Brenda was my first girlfriend. We were small children when we first started playing together, and as adolescence crept into our growing bodies I began to fall in love with her. By the time I was 11, I adored her. I loved her long, wavy brown hair and how it bounced on her shoulders when she walked. I loved her sparkling, dark eyes and the way she'd throw back her head and laugh at all my jokes. When she began to develop hips and breasts, I admired her maturity. Although I had never given her a ring, in my mind we were going steady. Every day we walked to school together, ate lunch together, and passed notes during class. Every afternoon I carried her books home. I thought we would go on like that forever.

One morning in 1969, during the first week of sixth grade, my whole life changed. The teacher had asked us to write a one-page essay on the natural habitat of the Canadian goose. As I began writing, my pencil point snapped on the page. I pushed back my wooden chair and walked up the aisle to the front of the class to wait in the pencil-sharpener line. I was thinking about what I would write, vaguely aware of the scraping of pencils, pages being turned in notebooks, the click-click of my teacher's high heels as she walked up and down the rows, and then the familiar touch of Brenda's elbow playfully digging into my side as she joined me in the line. I turned around and smiled at her. Something was going on. Her face looked different. She was beaming as she held up her hand and showed me a dime-store ring sitting prominently on her finger.

"It's from Neil," she whispered proudly. "We're going steady."

Her words slammed up against my heart cruelly, before settling in my brain. I could hear them circling around in my head as I tried to understand their meaning. My throat clamped shut and I swallowed hard, staring at Brenda in disbelief. My legs felt suddenly weak, and for a minute I thought I was going to faint. In an instant the ways of the world became clear to me. Brenda was going steady with Neil, not me. She was a girl. He was a boy. Until that moment, I had never questioned my childhood dream of growing up and marrying a woman. Suddenly everything was backwards. If what Brenda was saying was true, then I was supposed to go steady with boys too. I was 11 years old and no one had taught me about sex yet. My mind was not yet ingrained with the teachings of compulsory heterosexuality. This was my first moment of conscious indoctrination, and I was frightened to the bottom of my being. Somehow I turned away from her, sharpened my pencil, and went back to my seat, where I sat in a stupor for the rest of the morning. When the lunch bell rang, I charged out of class without waiting for Brenda and ran home, crying all the way. I told my mother I wasn't feeling well and stayed home for the rest of the day.

That night I barely slept. My mind was spinning; emotions were tearing at me from the inside out. I was trying to comprehend what had happened that day. Life had taken an unexpected turn. Everything looked different: the bedroom I shared with my sister, the trees on the street, my own face. My belly turned over and over, adrenaline ran through my veins; voices, words raced around in my head. I drifted in and out of sleep, while dreams I did not want to have overtook me. Images I did not know were there danced in the darkened room, like clowns mocking me. A bride in a white wedding gown walked down the aisle, her face covered by a veil. A man in a black tuxedo waited for her. The images moved closer, and I could see that the man's face was my face. He lifted the veil and the bride's face was mine also. The audience started yelling. "Men and women, boys and girls. Going steady. Neil and Brenda."

I woke up in a sweat, my heart pounding, my belly fluttering in fear. That night, I aged. In the morning when I woke up I could see it in my face. I could feel it in my bones. I was no longer a child, full of wonder, excitement, and innocence. I was almost a teenager, and what should have been some of the best years of my life were weighed down by the newfound knowledge that I was not right, that I was different somehow, that what I wanted I could not have. I did not have the words for what I was feeling but from that moment on I was troubled, and I knew there was no one I could talk to about it. There was no one who would understand.

After that day, Brenda and I drifted apart. She stopped walking to school with me and started walking with Neil. From then on, *he* carried her books home instead of me. We still saw each other, but things were never the same between us. I began to carefully watch her and the other girls around me, searching for clues on how to behave as a "real" girl. I tried to copy them as best I could, and from the age of 13 until the age of 18, I played at being straight. I went out on dates with boys. I let them kiss and touch me. I did what I was supposed to do. I have no clear memories of that time: My days as a heterosexual blur together into one prolonged, uncomfortable, backseat grope. Boys' clumsy hands under my shirt, sloppy kisses, heavy bodies, wet tongues, bumbling hands fumbling with clothes, and awkward, inept advances, pushing, pushing, always pushing at me for more.

I kissed the boys out of duty, and all the while I lusted after my new best friend, Rifka. I'd sit in her room watching her put on her makeup. As she sat on her bed in nothing but her underpants and bra, I tried not to look. I tried not to think about her later, in my bed at night, when my hand would find its way inside my pajamas. No one had specifically said that my feelings about her were wrong, but somehow I knew it was something I should keep to myself.

When I was 13, I started going to United Synagogue Youth, a Sunday afternoon social and cultural group for Jewish teenagers. There, I met Tova. We liked each other right away and became instant friends. She was more sophisticated and intelligent than most of my other girlfriends. She knew more about sex and drugs and life than I did, and I remember sometimes being in awe of her knowledge. Her mother was more lenient than mine, and she would let us smoke cigarettes and pot in their house. Tova was a wild kid, and together we had a lot of fun.

During that time I remember brainwashing myself.

"I'd rather have a boy than be one," I'd say, although it wasn't true. I was a baby butch, and I had no words, no context, no hope of being who I was. I was James Dean in a black leather jacket, leaning up against a brick city wall, one foot up behind me, cigarette dangling from my lips, hands thrust coolly inside my pockets. I was Mick Jagger, prancing across the stage, sexy in torn jeans and a tight T-shirt, crooning my rock and roll ballads to all the beautiful girls in the front row. I knew I wasn't a boy, but I felt like one. Deep inside I wanted what they wanted.

I tried to be straight. I really did. I even went out with a boy named Bruce for two years, faithfully schlepping him home for every family wedding, bar mitzvah, and funeral. Eventually we tried to have sex. I went on the pill and we waited until his parents were away for the weekend. Johnny Carson was on TV in the background. We undressed. We followed all the rules. Him on top. Me on bottom. In, out. In, out. It didn't feel particularly good. I was dry and uninspired. It hurt. I was grateful when it was over. We watched the rest of Johnny Carson. Charo was on that night, and I got more aroused watching her. Bruce drove me home, and I sat up all night thinking.

The next day I knew what I had to do. Over dinner at a Chinese restaurant, I broke up with him. He begged me to stay, but I had no feelings for him. I was 18, it was 1977, and I just couldn't fake it anymore. I gave him back his ring, kissed him on the cheek, and left him with the sweet-and-sour chicken balls. Walking out that door, I felt suddenly light, and I knew what I wanted to do next, although I didn't yet know why. I wanted to see Tova. Her image flashed into my head and refused to leave. We went to different high schools, and though I still considered her my friend, we hadn't seen each other in almost two years. The last time we had talked had been over the phone.

"What would you do," she had said, "if you found out one of your friends was doing something the rest of the world thought was wrong, but it felt really good and it wasn't hurting anyone?"

I shrugged. "If she's not hurting anyone else, I guess it's OK," I said.

"Yeah? That's good. I mean, is that how you really feel?"

"Uh...yeah...well, I mean, I guess it depends on what it is, you know." I was getting the feeling she was looking for something from me, but I had no idea what it was. For three hours we stayed on the phone, going back and forth this way, her trying to tell me something but not really saying anything. I had grown impatient.

"So what is it?" I pushed.

"Give me a second." She sounded angry.

"Come on, Tova. Whatever it is, it couldn't be that bad."

"Well, it's just that…" She sighed deeply. We were getting nowhere. I waited in silence. "It's just that…well, it's not like I'm sure or anything, but I think I might be…you know…gay."

As she said it, sirens rang in my body and my heart sped up.

"Oh…yeah?" I stammered. I went on to say something stupid like "That's OK with me" or "Hey, I still like you anyway." Whatever I said, it wasn't quite right and a gulf formed between us. Even over the phone, I could feel her pull away. One minute we were standing side by side; the next, a huge crack split the earth between us as we stood helplessly watching the ground underneath move in opposite directions until there was a deep canyon separating us. After that, Tova stopped calling me and I stopped calling her, until somehow two years went by with no contact.

I didn't know why Tova's image popped into my head the second I broke up with Bruce. I only knew that it did and I had to see her. I dialed her mother's number and found out that she had moved out on her own a few months earlier. I called her new number, and she invited me to come right over. When I knocked on her door, she opened it a crack.

"Before I let you in," she announced, "I want you to know that Dini and I are lovers."

Lovers. The word excited me, made me nervous. "Yeah," I tried to sound as casual as I could, "I know."

She opened the door wider and let me come inside. The gesture was to be the most significant one in my life since the pencil-sharpener incident. When Tova opened that door, it was the beginning of my journey back to myself, back to the little girl who knew she was going to grow up and marry a woman.

That night, Tova and Dini took me to my first gay bar.

The Studio, in downtown Toronto, was rumored to have been run by the Mafia. During the week it was a major motion picture distribution office. On weekends it was a gay bar. By coincidence, that first time I went it was Halloween night. All over the three-story building were dozens of unusually tall Barbara Streisands, Diana Rosses, and Tina Turners. I found out the following week that on a regular Saturday night there would be only a handful of drag queens, but on that first night the place was full of them. From the moment they checked our IDs and we walked through the doors, I loved it. In the Studio, I was Dorothy and this was the Land of Oz. I was Alice and this was Wonderland. Although technically I was still straight, I didn't feel out of place. I felt like I belonged there, among the tall queens and the tough butches; the flannel-shirted, overall-wearing, short-haired, androgynous women; and the thin disco boys in their too-tight pants. Standing against the wall, watching men dance with men, women with women, I felt as if someone had opened the blinds and I was seeing into a whole new world—but one that was familiar somehow. It was as if it had always been there, only out of focus. That night, undefined images became sharp, while long-buried feelings inside me began to stir, preparing for their journey to the surface.

I began to spend most of my free time with Tova and Dini, going to the bar, hanging out at their apartment, getting high, and talking about how we were going to change the world. Sometimes I worried that I was crowding them, but they didn't seem to mind. I didn't think about it too much, but if you had asked me I'd have said I was still straight. One day, however, that changed. The transition must have been gradual, but I remember it as happening all at once. I was alone with Tova, and when I looked into her eyes I was aware of something different. I was feeling attracted to her, drawn to her. When she looked at me, it was with a new intensity, and her gaze made my belly flip. Her eyes were not just eyes anymore. They took on a dreamy quality, and I could almost jump inside and drown in them.

Every time I was around Tova after that night, I had trouble breathing, I was restless, my senses were heightened. When she accidentally brushed against me, my body reacted. I wanted her to touch me and would make up excuses for her to do so, like asking her to pass the salt or ketchup. I knew I was in love with her, but how could it be? Wasn't I straight? Wasn't Tova in love with Dini? How could I be in love with this friend I had known so long? How could I be in love with someone who already had a lover? How could I break up their home? I was disgusted with myself and was sure these feelings were my own. I had no idea until much later that Dini was attracted to me too.

For the next few weeks, I stayed away from her. I was scared of my strange new feelings, and I ran from them. I was so removed from myself after years of playing straight that I made no connection with my long-lost childhood dreams. And yet, the whole time I stayed away I thought of no one but her. When she finally called to ask where I'd been and to invite me over, the sound of her voice penetrated deep into my heart, and I knew that whatever was going to happen between us could not be stopped. Deep in my soul I knew it was my destiny. False ethics and learned behavior were trying to rule my life, but in the end the force of my body would win out. The little baby butch who dreamed of finding a princess of her own was back on her horse. The hinges on the drawbridge that had been sealed shut all those years ago in the pencil-sharpener line were beginning to loosen. If I had listened closely, I could have heard them squeak.

I put down the phone, slipped into a pair of baggy green army pants, pulled on my work boots and my best flannel shirt, and caught a bus to her place. When I arrived, I was surprised to find her alone. Dini had gone to spend time with her mother. I went inside and sat on the couch with Tova. We were both extremely nervous. Sexual energy was flowing freely throughout the apartment. Whenever I'd look into her eyes, a warm feeling started in my body and spread throughout my body. Cloud nine could not even begin to describe how happy I felt just to be with her. I imagined taking her in my arms and kissing her, but I wasn't sure how to get there. For hours we talked, dancing around the issue, looking meaningfully into each other's eyes but not saying anything about it. Finally, by accident, our fingers touched. We grabbed hands and held on. In slow motion, without a word, we moved toward each other. I saw her lips moving closer to mine. It seemed to take forever, and then we were kissing. Her kiss was softer than I'd ever imagined. I pulled her down onto me, and I plunged through a time zone. Her body against mine brought back old memories, forgotten dreams. I was home. I was right back where I'd started from. I was me again. I was a prince, and she was my princess. I was a knight in shining armor, and she was my queen. We kissed for hours and then slowly undressed each other. My body delighted in her touch. After years spent playing at being straight, faking it with boys, I had no idea that sex could feel so good. All night long we made love, and as we did, I crossed a line. I traversed centuries, and I knew I would never be the same again: Baby butch returns in all her glory. Someone had turned on the light at the end of the tunnel, and I could finally see my way clear.

Somewhere in the back of my mind I knew that what we were doing was not honorable. Tova was cheating on Dini, and I was colluding. We were young and reckless, and our actions had no consequences then. When you're that age, you live in the moment, and that moment was all body and no mind. That moment was passion and lust, and we couldn't have stopped it if we had tried. I could have died then and it would have been the happiest day of my life. I had grown up, and even if I hadn't married a woman, I was, at least, kissing one.

Learning to Speak

Bev Clark

My family calls me Pooks, but my real name is Beverley. Mostly I call myself Bev. My mother named me Pooks and it stuck. She told me I didn't speak until I was 3, and when I did, I stuttered. I didn't need words to get what I wanted; pointing nearly always did the trick—even then I wasn't sure that people wanted to hear what I had to say.

My siblings and I joked that our parents did it three times and we were the results. Beryl, my mother, was born in Fort Beaufort, a dusty, one-horse South African town. Donald Arthur Clark, my father, was an immigrant to South Africa looking to leave behind the hopelessness and certain poverty that Scotland offered him.

When my mother was 22, she and two girlfriends decided to get all their teeth taken out. Apparently it was the "in" thing to do. I can imagine them, arm in arm, laughing like drains as they made their way to the dentist's office and emerged as "new women." Whenever I was down in the dumps my mother would flip out her false teeth and roll her eyes. We'd start laughing, and my dark mood would be broken.

Besides being armed with a flash set of falsies, my mother sported a few other eccentricities. In a country like South Africa, where the heat would drive old and young alike into the nearest puddle for relief, not being able to swim was very unusual. Old photographs show my mother wrapped up in a long-sleeve blouse and baggy slacks sitting patiently on a Cape beach waiting for her husband and children to finish playing in the sea. Her dislike of the sun left her limbs alabaster white.

My mother also didn't drive. A couple of driving lessons with my father left her a complete wreck—the Buicks and Anglias in which she practiced didn't escape unscathed either. I think my parents' relationship went into reverse around this time. And having a mother that didn't swim or drive was difficult for a kid who wanted to fit in.

My father's wanderlust didn't stop after he'd moved to South Africa. After a while he became bored, or things just didn't work out—things often didn't work out for him—and he'd move on to new enterprises. My memories of him are confused: I admired him, because he was so adventurous, always exploring new territory. His brush with death from contracting malaria, a broken neck from playing rugby, and an enrollment in the British South African Police all added to my hero worship. But I also felt pity for him because nothing ever seemed to work out for him. When he excitedly suggested to my mother that they move to Rhodesia, the land of opportunity, so he could make his fortune in gold mining, she prepared herself for yet another half-attempt at a new beginning.

* * *

West View was on the corner of Prince Edward Street and Baines Avenue. Apparently, Thomas Baines, a famous painter, arrived at Victoria Falls in 1862 with "a gun in one hand and a paintbrush in the other." This was the first block of flats that we lived in when we moved to Salisbury, Rhodesia. Predictably, after a few years in Rhodesia, my father gave up on his get-rich-quick scheme. Coaxing gold from rocks deep in the earth in Matabeleland was less glamorous than it had been in his dreams, and he was ready to move on. My mother, however, wouldn't budge. So my brother Craig and I ended up staying in Rhodesia with my mother. I watched my father drive off with my 13-year-old sister for the long journey to Johannesburg.

My first few years at junior school were uneventful and, by default, good ones, although a few things set me apart from the average Rhodesian teenager. For instance, I walked four kilometers each day to school under huge, flamboyant trees that reached up toward the cloudless blue sky. Most of my friends lived with both a mother and a father, and I seemed to be the only child who lived in a flat. I always felt ashamed about where I lived. My double life started early, and even now it's still hard to shake off. Still, I blended in with the sea of green uniforms and was grateful to be just another one of the girls. But things changed when the bell rang at lunchtime and when weekends rolled around. I felt unsure and embarrassed about inviting friends back to our flat, which left me unable to move beyond my dismal borders.

The afternoons were long and lonely. I mooched about in the West View gardens, kicking up dust, taking grasshoppers captive, and scaring lizards into losing their shiny tails. I felt so alone. The words to describe my dreams and fears withered in my throat, and as I grew older my silence deepened. Little did I know that "normal" family structures would be reshaped by the Rhodesian War. Young husbands on extended call-ups returned to find that the distance that had grown between them and their wives was too difficult to bridge. Soldiers, who had seen and been involved in the terrible atrocities of war, returned as shadows of their former selves, unrecognizable to their families. The soaring number of deaths would catapult many of my friends into one-parent families.

I never really knew how my mother handled my father leaving, since I was only 9 years old at the time. Mostly, she just got on with things and tried to make life comfortable and safe for us. My father's departure signaled the end of her marriage and she found herself alone in a strange city, jobless and loaded with debt accrued by my father. Lawyers regularly sent her letters threatening all sorts of nastiness. We had so little money that life became unbearable at times and my mother's pain and desperation was difficult to bear. She broke down one night when our electricity had been cut off because she couldn't pay the bill. While I hunched over my homework in flickering candlelight, she sat in an apologetic and defeated lump in front of me, crying softly. There was no food or electricity, and there were bills to pay.

My mother's moods were viciously unpredictable, but she never took her frustration or anger out on us. Whenever she felt particularly sad she waltzed me around the kitchen, pressing my face deep into her enormous bosom as she held on to me tightly and tried to encourage my unwilling feet to match her rhythm. The tune that always lifted her spirits was "My Way," sung by Shirley Bassey, whom she completely adored. My mother knew all the words and felt as though the song had been written especially for her.

At home, my mother's only other adult company and help was our domestic worker, Grace. She ironed in the kitchen, swaying to the sounds of the Doobie Brothers singing "Ooo hoo hoo, Miss Grace." My mother went to work early in the morning and returned in the evening, so Grace kept an eye on us when we got back from school. If I ran riot she would purse her lips, let out a long, slow whistle, muttering, "*Aikona*[1], Miss Pookie, don't *shupa*[2] me now."

At school the girls had to knit either *balaclavas* (hats) or blankets for the "boys on the border" fighting in the Rhodesian War. I was completely hopeless at knitting and my mother didn't have the time, so Grace knitted an olive-green *balaclava* for me. Only later did I realize the irony of my request. Grace lived in a *kia*[3] at the back of our block of flats and I spent a lot of time there. Dog-eared photographs decorated the walls, reminding Grace of her other life in the rural areas where she returned on her annual leave. While she looked after two little white kids in Salisbury, a relative looked after Tendai, her son. She only saw him three weeks a year. Rhodesia was a country divided by race and class, but in our home these divisions didn't exist. My mother's early influence allowed me to grow up sensitive to the inequities and horrors of racism.

A new girl joined my class at school, and we liked each other straight away. Martina Reitbauer was blond and chubby. Her body promised better things in the years to come; already her breasts were noticeable under her green uniform. She had pretty hands and sculptured nails, lacquered with clear-white nail varnish. She always looked neat and tidy, her long hair tied back in an intricate French plai. Next to her, I looked messy. Martina lived with her mother and stepfather in a double-story house on Cleveland Avenue. She had an odd-sounding foreign name that no one could pronounce, which set her apart. It seemed natural that we would be friends.

In the afternoons I'd lie on my bed and listen to my two records. The sun filtered through the lace curtains my mother had insisted on hanging so that dangerous black men couldn't peer in. I daydreamed the afternoons away. My eccentric record collection included an LP of marching songs and ABBA's greatest hits. The ABBA record cover showed a photo of Bjorn and Agnetha kissing. This picture fascinated me, and I'd lie on my back for hours listening to their songs and gazing at their lips so tightly pressed together. My other record cover pictured long-legged drum majorettes in boots and very short skirts twirling their batons; I also couldn't stop looking at them.

Martina and I started going out with boys. I'd been getting more and more sexually curious, but my exploration had been limited to awkward attempts at self-stimulation with a golf ball. I was ready for something else. Carl was a tall, thin boy who wore baggy shorts. At school, we played marbles at break time. He told me he had always fancied me, and we kissed whenever we had the chance. At Blakiston there was a creepy, dark, underground shed where we parked our bikes every morning. Carl would wait for me there and we'd quickly press our mouths together and feel very grown up. He also helped me with my swimming, since unfortunately I had inherited my mother's defective aquatic genes. Although I could do just about every other sport, I sank like a stone when I got in the pool. Each kid was given a certificate of competence if they could swim one length unaided. When the weaker swimmers attempted their first full length, a good swimmer had to swim beside them to make sure they were safe. My turn finally came, and Carl, who was an ace swimmer, encouraged me down the length of the pool, thus sealing our love. I remember Martina and I went to his house one day. He had a few friends over, and we all ended up naked in his bedroom, giggling and fiddling with each other. I was flat on my back with either Carl or Robert's willy wiggling in front of my mouth. Both Martina and I were laughing our heads off, but the boys were quite serious.

"Made you look, made you look, made you kiss a kaffir cook." I grew up in Rhodesia being looked after by black women and waited on by black people. Every black person I came across was in a subservient position. At school, all of the teachers and students were white. Through the fence, snotty-faced *picanins*[4] watched us play sports. They were on the outside looking in. I was on the inside, but my feelings of inadequacy made me feel like an outsider. As I looked across the playing fields, my isolation and loneliness deepened like the afternoon shadows creeping across the grass.

I remember teachers talking in hushed tones when we arrived at school one morning. Apparently, graffiti had been scrawled across one of the pristine white walls. FUCK KAFFIRS in big black letters screamed at us. I think everyone was more shocked by the *f* word than anything else. The racism and prejudice ignited in the homes of my white friends was stoked in our classrooms and on our playing fields. At school we were fed a diet of Rhodesian patriotism. I remember my class sitting on wooden benches in a darkened room listening to a tape dramatizing the Shangani uprising. We huddled in groups, our knees pressed together in excitement, transfixed by the desperate voices of the white men as they fought off the natives. It was difficult not to be seduced by it all.

Those old colonial battles, which are a part of our history, didn't seem so long ago as the halcyon days of white rule succumbed to the wave of discontent rising in the black community. Fear settled heavily in our stomachs when we heard that white people were being assaulted and murdered. The news on the radio described how a houseboy had slipped into an old white woman's bedroom and strangled her with his belt. My mother's mouth twisted in worry when she heard these stories. Should she stay in Rhodesia or take us back to South Africa before things got worse?

My sister, Debbie, returned from South Africa and got a job as a tele-ad girl at the *Rhodesia Herald,* where she quickly made friends with a woman named Cathy. The two of them were regularly threatened with dismissal because they smoked *dagga*[5] on their breaks and hardly ever got the ads right.

Soon after, Debbie proudly prepared me for my first day of high school. Unfortunately, my face had erupted into a repulsive assortment of pimples, but Debbie rose to the challenge and did her best to cover them with foundation. She scraped my hair into two very tight, perky pigtails. Debbie's face was a picture of concentration as she struggled to get them level. Next she jammed a boater on my head that inched slowly upward as my pigtails asserted their independence. I had to push it down every five seconds, until I finally gave up and kept one hand permanently on my head.

My sister and I made our way down Salisbury Street to Girls' High School. She clipped along in her high heels and I dragged my feet reluctantly down a path I was certain I'd hate. Jacaranda trees lined our way, and bunches of lavender flowers lay plump with air in them, their voluptuousness fading as the day got warmer.

My high school years were clouded by the Rhodesian War. I remember returning for the third term one year and seeing Shirley Wicksteed laboriously pushing herself around in a wheelchair. She and her sister Kerry lived on a farm. During the holidays an innocent jaunt on the back of a trailer ended with a land mine shattering her legs and her life. Kerry still skipped around school, her beautiful brown legs a stark reminder of what her sister had lost.

Then one day a girl named Vicki arrived, dragging half her young body from classroom to classroom. Her smile had no light left in it, and she didn't know what to do with her anger. Shirley could at least direct hers at the "blacks," but Vicki's tragedy was the result of a white soldier's carelessness. A ricocheting bullet came to rest in Vicki's neck and now half of her body was dead. Constant reminders of war surrounded us.

* * *

Most afternoons, Martina and I went to the Les Brown pool to tan. We hoped to find a boyfriend there and tried our best to be alluring in our skimpy bikinis. Martina managed to turn many heads, especially those of the middle-aged Portuguese men who lounged about looking for young conquests. When the summer thunderstorms interrupted our visits to the pool, we curled up on the couch at Martina's house and looked for the dirty bits in her mother's enormous collection of paperbacks.

Back at school, kids joked that every Thursday was "lesbi day." We laughed, joked, and nudged each other in embarrassment, not really sure why we were making fun of it. Although I was surrounded by many teachers who went by "Miss" and whose one concession to femininity was a slash of bright-red lipstick, I really hadn't thought about lesbianism at all, especially since Martina and I were both sold on boys. Our bench at the back of the science room had an impressive list of names scratched into the wood. The fact that some of the boys were yet to even smile in our direction didn't worry us much. But things changed when I went on a countrywide basketball tour.

After playing a match against a school in the Eastern Highlands, our team spent the night in their boarding hostel. With a couple of friends I decided to sneak into Miss Rogers's room. Our coach had always interested me, and I wanted to see what she did at night. Leading the pack, I slowly opened her door and inched over the old wooden floorboards. It took awhile for my eyes to adjust to the darkness, but soon I saw two people making out in the single bed in the corner of the room. Their moans were muffled under the sheets and blankets. My friends behind me insisted on having a look, but I backed out, hoping we wouldn't be noticed. Unfortunately, the floorboards let out a long, slow squeak. We ran for it.

Later, I discovered that Lauren, a friend of mine, had been in bed with Miss Rogers. I was completely intrigued. On the bus back to Salisbury I kept sneaking looks at Lauren, wondering what was going on with her and wanting to talk to her about what I'd seen. The idea of two women being sexual with each other had never crossed my mind before that night, and I desperately wanted to know more.

* * *

It's funny how things happen in life. One minute you're walking this straight, narrow, predictable path, and suddenly a new experience leads you down a completely different road. Soon after the basketball trip, I became friendly with Brenda, who was one of my teachers. She was young, approachable, and gorgeous. Our friendship turned into a mellow and gentle courtship; after a few months we experienced that first kiss that's so special it blows you away. My years of lonely afternoons gave way to delicious hours of sexual exploration in another woman's arms. Years of struggling to find the right words to describe my feelings and thoughts ended when I allowed this special person to get close to me. The flat that I had been ashamed of for so long became a sanctuary in which we could safely be with each other.

The Salvation Army headquarters was a couple of blocks away from the flat. The melodies of their band filtered into my room while my hands and mouth traveled the length of Brenda's body. We laughed when the trumpets punctuated a particularly "moral point." Finally, I belonged, and it all felt so right.

NOTES

1. Watch out!
2. Bother me
3. Usually one small room with an outside toilet
4. Children
5. Marijuana

Sweating, Thumping, Telling

Gillian Hanscombe

I'm sitting at a double desk (replete with two removable white porcelain inkwells being filled from a large bottle by the ink monitor), second to the back row, in an Australian state school classroom. It's 1952, and I'm 7 years old. Diagonally behind me sits Glenys Hill, who taps me on the shoulder, wanting to borrow a pencil. I turn around. With what I later learn from books is a thumping heart, I think in words, *I love Glenys Hill!*

Then I'm 9, walking round the back of the girls' shelter-shed, where we eat packed lunches, arm in arm with Terrie Fisher. I say to her, "I love you." She says, "Do you mean like a man loves a woman?" *Oh, yes,* I'm about to say. *Oh, yes.* But she goes on, "Or like a friend loves a friend." I say "yes" to that, knowing nothing, but somehow knowing this second yes is the correct yes.

Next I'm 12. I've gone to a fee-paying girls' school run by Church of England nuns, where my mother had been a boarder 30 years before. I'm entranced by a bigger girl deigning to talk to me. She's called Maxine and is frightfully strong. She's 14 and hits tennis balls harder than anyone in school. She teaches me to hit tennis balls too, every morning before school (I get up at 7 to be there for as long as possible), and every afternoon (my mother rages when I'm not home until 8 at night). Our fingers touch as we sway about, standing squashed together in the athletics team bus. I sweat and thump like anything. She writes me hugely long letters, hugely long poems in the style of Tennyson, Milton, and the

Shakespeare of the history plays, though I won't know the originals until much later. We "wrestle" in the cloakrooms. She calls it wrestling and she always wins, but I don't mind a bit being pinned down by her. "I love you," she says fiercely against my sweating ear, my burning head held hard down flat on the concrete. The other girls snigger when they catch us, but I'm only dimly aware that they don't do these things.

It's the holidays. I spend a week at Maxine's house. Both her parents go to work, so we're alone. We spend all day in bed, hugging and kissing, declaring passion, kissing some more. We don't take our clothes off and don't know what else to do, other than kissing and hugging.

After a year, my mother confronts me. She's found my shoeboxes filled with Maxine's letters and poems. She burns them all. She's worried about me. On the advice of the family doctor, a woman, my mother makes me join a mixed church fellowship and a mixed dancing class. I get crushes on the young woman who runs the church fellowship and on one of the girls at the dancing class, but I don't tell anyone. I kiss all the boys who want to kiss me, but my heart never thumps. I only care that one or the other of them kisses me, so I can pass with the other girls.

I fall in love with God for a while and then with my English teacher, who's 22. I'm 15, and she spends time with me out of school, telling me about modern poetry and herself. We hug and kiss a lot, but she won't let me take her clothes off. I vaguely want to, though. My father thinks this friendship is "unhealthy" and gets my mother to send me to see the doctor again. The doctor prescribes more "mixed" activities and activity in general.

Then I'm 16 and in my last year of school. My heart thumps again. She's called Patsie and is a boarder at a different school. We've met on and off for years when our schools have played each other at tennis, softball, basketball, and so on. We make friends and write letters. She spends a boarders' weekend with me. I stay at her house over the holidays, and we lie in bed together, declaring love and passion. One night she says "I don't think either of us has any inhibitions" and slips her hand down my pajama waist, down my belly, down to my pubic hair. I do the same to her. I wonder what all the sticky wet is, having no idea. We rub a lot...

Her mother phones my mother. She's opened a letter I posted to Patsie. She says to my mother, "I've never *seen* such a letter in my life. I would never write such a letter to my own husband." "And she has five children," my mother explains to me, dreadfully distressed. I can't make it out. My letter had words in it like *breasts* and *hair* and *thighs*. Wanting them, that is. Wanting Patsie. Don't wives want their husbands, then? Patsie's mother doesn't seem to. My mother doesn't seem to either. Women don't?

I'm sent to another doctor. She says it will all pass. She says I should meet more boys. I've already met all the boys the other girls have met. "Meet more then," she says heartily.

Later, I'm sent for psychoanalysis. I do that for four years and it makes me better and stronger and saner. During that time, I have Kerryn and Ruth and Kate and others... By now I know the word *lesbian* (it's in the books) and the word *orgasm* (it's in the same books), and I've had sex with men, but it never once made my heart thump.

I'm 23 and living with a lover called D. We plan to go to Europe and live in England for a bit. She's a musician. I want to travel and write, but what I really want to do is get away with being a lesbian. A couple of years later, on a visit back home, I talk to my mother. She worries all the time about my being "alone" and "not settled" in England. "I'm not alone," I tell her. "If you're going to worry, it may as well be about something true rather than not true. D is my lover. We live together and sleep together. I'm a lesbian. I'm not alone."

My mother mourns. She's a Christian and thinks it's wrong and that she's wrong and what did she do wrong?

"Nothing," I tell her, but it's no use. She mourns and worries and blames herself. But she doesn't change toward me.

Three years later my mother dies suddenly. I plan to have a baby and become pregnant. I lose that baby and try again, this time successfully. I learn about feminism and gay liberation. I join things, start writing differently, and feel better and better about being lesbian. But I'm not too sure I can pinpoint my coming out. If you live like a lesbian before you know the word, it all just feels like going on and growing up.

How I Learned to Write Love Letters and Eventually Got Girls

Bonnie J. Morris

"God, you're such a romantic!" says my current girl-friend, L.B., who's been deluged with my love letters since our moonlit courtship at the Michigan Womyn's Music Festival. "Date a writer and you'll get letters," I told her, but lately I've been wrestling with that fine autobiographical question: Which came first, my identity as a writer or my crushes on girls? How much of my writing life has been one long love letter to a series of beloved girls? When did I first take pen in hand to say: *I love, I want*? Maybe it's the nudge of turning 40, but suddenly my childhood coming-out has seemed important to understand. And so, during Rosh Hashana last autumn, L.B. and I went to visit my old neighborhood in Los Angeles, to take photographs of the places where I wrote my first love letters to older girls during elementary school.

I was one empowered little kid. At the age of 3, according to my parents, I climbed the giant magnolia tree in our front yard and sat there shouting "I've got the power!" at startled passersby. Climbing the tree was perhaps my sole athletic gesture in a childhood entirely constructed around language; I came down from the tree, went into the house, and began inscribing my life on paper. So while I was not a physical tomboy, I identified with tomboy characters in kids' books, and relished as a role model any scrappy little girl who questioned adult authority. My two heroines were Harriet from *Harriet the Spy* and Scout in *To Kill a Mockingbird*. No one ever told me that the authors of these two transformative, empowering books were lesbians. What might it have meant to me if I'd known, earlier, that my self-selected favorite authors were dykes?

While other baby dykes spent their childhoods playing ball with boys, I was a bookworm and a writer, coming home every day to write stories after school. I wrote on the living room floor or at the kitchen table in our house on Kelton Avenue. As I attended a progressive multicultural public school that enrolled kids from all over the world, I wrote about girls in other lands, girls of different religious and ethnic backgrounds from mine, girls facing socioeconomic troubles I'd never encountered. When my mother occasionally ordered me to put down the pen and go out and play, I wandered dreamily in our backyard, touching the ivy, daisies, and moonflowers, and imagined that I ran an international school for girls; in my head I wrote out long lists of their names. I had an imaginary woman friend who lived in the telephone, pen pals in Wales and Hawaii, a collection of ethnically costumed international dolls, and I belonged to a Campfire Girl troop that boasted members from India and Israel, and from Jewish, Japanese, Filipina, and Mexican heritages. I saw, every day of my life, the beauty of girls and women of every skin tone, nationality, and language, and my earliest stories embraced this ideal, much to the delight of my ethnically intermarried parents.

My mother watched me produce an enormous amount of work as a child, and began saving my stories from the time I could write. It's to her credit that I possess, to this day, a photocopy of the love letter I sent to my baby-sitter, Diane, when I was 7 years old. My mother thought the letter was sweet, and mimeographed it for posterity before mailing it from her secretarial position at UCLA. I had cried and cried when Diane moved away, and when I wrote to her it was to declare, "I love you! Yes, yes, I do love you. I DO!!!!" with a rather precocious drawing of the baby-sitter, portrayed in bikini and shades, holding out a towel to me on the beach at Malibu, and me thinking (as written in a balloon above my head) *Diane, I wish I had you!*

This document hangs framed in my bedroom today. I want to be reminded of that impulse, that free agency experienced as a child, that unself-conscious declaration of love, my first love letter to an older girl.

All well and good. But by the time I garnered the nerve to tell another girl I liked her, at age 9, I had become a less empowered kid. By then, I honestly felt like an oddball: I read at college level, discussed politics, attended antiwar demonstrations and vigils with my parents, and was not remotely interested in playing dolls or house or any of the other girl games designed to promote a love of domestic toil. I interacted awkwardly with the neighborhood kids my own age and sat in my father's chair reading Langston Hughes and Harper Lee while my peers galloped through the house pretending to be the Partridge family. The more I lived in my own head, in a world of ideas, the more I grew painfully aware that little girls in my culture were defined externally by cuteness and praised according to the feminine behaviors they exhibited through gendered playground games. An interest in *ideas* hardly sufficed as girlish, particularly since smart girls represented a threat to male supremacy. Cute little girls supposedly refreshed, rather than challenged, the grown-ups around them by representing playful innocence instead of engaging in discussions on racism or Vietnam. I knew I was "different."

Also by age 9, I was encountering the first critiques of my growing girlchild body—adult authority figures suggested that I was a little chubby and that my overbite would require correction in the near future. For the first time I began to feel unattractive, in need of repair, lacking this and having too much of that. The possibility of social failure due to physical appearance, which haunts every woman in this sexist society, now placed me into a parenthesis of competition I did not understand. Concerns about body image cut into valuable writing time. I was expected to work at looking good; all women were. Bailing out of the race toward qualifying for cheerleader meant that one had lazily conceded to nerd status—and, by extension, downward mobility, as female success (in the 1960s) still depended upon looking good to high-powered men.

Even though my parents were involved in the Movement and were critical of many middle-class values, in practice they wanted me to be pretty and popular for my coming 1970s adolescence. I did not yet grasp that my Aryan looks lent me privileges my Jewish mother, a first-generation American, had never enjoyed. I had my father's Protestant last name too. Cultivating these advantages would permit me to gain entry to events and institutions previously closed to my own mother. Maintaining that WASP edge, however, was going to require endless dieting, moderating my naturally loud voice and exuberant mannerisms, wearing of braces and dresses, and pandering to the white god of assimilation, lest those errant immigrant genes burst forth in a nonhomogenized frenzy. Slowly I internalized the message that the healthy, strong flesh on my body was not cute, whereas in my mother's generation, and to thousands of other immigrant families like hers, a kid who looked well-fed and was at the top of her class was a symbol of success and good luck in golden America.

The point of all this is that I grasped clearly that many adults (and, indeed, other children) had tolerated my prolific writing and imaginative word play as long as I was a cute little girl. That era was about to end. I was light-haired and light-skinned, which gave me a *lot* of privilege in society, but my girl-identified world would soon be shaped by new standards concerning weight, figure, breasts, and submissive demeanor, and I didn't want to play.

When the school year began in the fall of 1970, I was

promoted from third grade to an experimental fifth-grade classroom. I was one of eight younger brainy kids mixed in with a dazzling surfeit of 10-year-olds. I sat with, and befriended, the older girls in the class—who were sloppy and self-conscious and Jewish like me—recognizing, in their nervous comedy routines, the ancient tactics of Yiddish humor as protective armor. I knew that our sarcastic banter placed us apart from the glamorous, unruffled girls who showcased a composed Christian femininity. Though I might profess contempt for the ideology that declared those girls to be more desirable, more worthy of admiration, I found I had internalized the very standard I opposed. I, too, wanted the attention and acceptance of popular girls—and I no longer identified as a girl myself.

That year when I first had a negative image of myself, I fell in love with the girl in my classroom who most resembled the white media's definition of gorgeous. She was a cool blond blue-eyed 10-year-old I'll call Randi; feminine, regal, dignified, utterly beyond correction. No one on the playground dared approach her. I had by this time enjoyed crushes on various baby-sitters and camp counselors, but this was *different*. Randi was a schoolgirl like me, someone I saw every day. The prolonged proximity lent an intensity to feelings I had never experienced before. In firm black ballpoint pen, I wrote "I love Randi" inside a red-and-white heart on my calendar.

As a grubby 9-year-old, fully one year younger than the unattainable goddess, I resigned myself to gazing from afar. This might have continued forever had our egalitarian teacher not stepped in to announce a new seating plan whereby we could request our own deskmates. I had been sitting next to my friend Sheila for years in school but let such old loyalties fly right down the freeway and, in secret, wrote a long note to my teacher, begging her to seat me with Randi. Please. Please. Please.

I took a great risk in spewing out my tortured inner emotions to the adult who controlled this "gifted" class. It so happened that this particular teacher was gentle, good-humored, and living with another woman, although of course I didn't know that at the time. When we arrived at school the next day, I found that the entire classroom had been rearranged so that I was partnered with Randi. Joy. Rapture. Access. There was her long blond hair shining at my elbow, and I had no idea what to say. We studied in silence. And then one day she raised her head to ask me casually, "What does this word mean?" It would be our only exchange for weeks.

I watched her sweep confidently around the playground at recess, her arms interlocked with the arms of her two best friends. The curious thing was that I didn't really want to be *like* Randi. She was never able to demean herself by clowning for an audience, as I so enjoyed doing. She both benefited from and was limited by her image—the good-girl, super-femme image projected onto her by adults and adoring schoolmates like me. I had far more leeway in my life and played a greater range of characters, vacillating from good girl to outrageous smart-ass on my daily trapeze. Ultimately, I had to admit that there was no logical premise operating here. Like thousands of crushed-out radical schoolgirls before me, I was simply pining away for a rather stunning babe. Why justify it?

Finally, I took action. During recess one day, I sat at a lunch table and wrote Randi a long love note, begging her to be mine, explaining that all I really wanted was to walk on the playground with our arms linked. I left this letter on Randi's chair, assuming she'd read it when she came in from recess. But when I reentered the classroom later, some kindly girl took me aside and gave me the bad news: The boys in our class had found and read my love note. They had added rude comments, crossed off my name, and then signed the name of the least attractive boy in class. I was sick. Not only did every kid in the room now know that I loved Randi, but *my* romantic love letter, *my* writing, had been ascribed to a boy.

I promptly wrote another letter, ordering Randi to meet me in front of the principal's office at lunchtime. This time I made sure Randi herself took the note from her seat. She looked at me, gave me an assertive, conspiratorial nod—and *whee,* did I feel powerful again. But what, exactly, did I want to say to her? What sort of speech should I prepare? She would expect me to explain why I had requested an audience with her during valuable lunch time. If only I chose my words effectively, I might convince her to be my friend.

When we stood, alone, in the corridor at the front of the school at noon, I paced about, trembling, and offered her a stick of gum. Then I blew any pretense of cool, and kneeling down before her, said, "Randi, you're my hero." In the great tradition of courtly behavior, though I had yet to study the romantic love tradition of medieval knighthood, I said to her, "Allow me to be a member of your court." If I'd had a cape, I would have laid it at her feet.

Throughout my flowery speech of love, patched together from every book I'd ever read, Randi stood tall and still, obviously uncomfortable but unwilling to walk away from my stream of declarations. Finally, I dared to explain that it was I who had put that first note on her chair, not some boy, and, marvelously unflappable, she gazed down at me and replied, serenely, "Oh, I knew that was from you—I know you like me." She looked 18 rather than 10 right then, and I thought, *Wow! She knows.*

We parted without further ado, and though I felt I had shocked her in some way, she seemed to chalk it all up to my immaturity as a 9-year-old. Personally, I was delighted to have placed my feelings out in the open. I don't remember any more than this—just the shouts of the other kids on the playground sounding so distant, Randi's height and unnervingly beautiful face, and the sense that I had at last made some sort of daring attempt at a contact with another girl.

Hours later the bell rang to release us from school, and I went over to the racks to retrieve my bicycle. I pedaled down the street thoughtfully and suddenly saw Randi walking alone. "Hi, Bonnie," she greeted me and then gave me a truly intimate, private, knowing smile. It was a smile I would come to know very well as a grown-up—a smile that says, *Oh, yeah, stuff went down between you and me.* I arrived home delirious with the thrill of having been recognized and acknowledged as a suitor. I believe I told my mother, "This is a red-letter day for me."

Nothing really changed after that. Randi already had two best friends. But soon my parents told me that at the end of that school year our family would be moving to North Carolina, and the spring of 1971 saw the sale of our old house. Because I was leaving Los Angeles forever, Randi generously invited me to perform in a class play that she and her two best friends had written. This allowed me to attend a cast party in Randi's garden on the last day of school, and from these activities I summoned the courage to ask Randi over to my house. There, amid the packing boxes and crates, I finally maneuvered Randi into my father's chair and sat with one arm around her, showing her my favorite books. My mother walked by, observed us squashed into one armchair with others comfortably empty, and gave me a look that would become familiar later in life. And that day was the last time I ever saw Randi. I walked her home, stood clumsily on the patch of clover near her front walk, and slowly backed away. I didn't know how to touch or embrace her in farewell.

All of that happened 30 years ago; and it's a piece of my coming-out history I've never told before. I went on to write many, many love letters to other girls, some more gladly received than others, and by age 13, when I began keeping a journal, my writing and my love of girls were so intertwined that they paved a solid highway for my life. I realize now that my writing life and writing identity came first, because I had a vocabulary of love for the years before I physically matured—before I knew how to "make my move" or understood what girls might do in bed. With love letters and poems, I took an active, even aggressive, role in wooing, as a kid, and thus language, more than sex, made me the lesbian I am today.

And so, I did go back to visit my old neighborhood. I spent a long sweet weekend in Los Angeles, my first time back in many years, and made my girlfriend, L.B., drive past my old house. Tentatively I knocked on the door, wanting only to see the rooms where I once wrote. I found that two lesbians own the house; they live where I grew bold and eat at a table near the place I once wrote to my baby-sitter. They make love in the bedroom where I dreamed.

L.B. and I then drove over to my elementary school. I pretended I just wanted to take a quick look, but I knew what I needed to do, this time, in one great symbolic ritual. It was late in the day and the schoolkids were gone, and so there in the corridor by the main office, where I once knelt in front of Randi, I took my new lover in my arms and kissed her long and well. Thirty years had passed, and I stood on that same square of concrete, big and proud, on Rosh Hoshanah eve, a homecoming to the girl within.

These days my love letters are confident and sure, and do result in kissing. I grew up to be myself, only more so.

Sharpshooter

Marcie Just

Another school year was beginning and with it the transfer to senior high. It was 1965 in East St. Louis, and my primary concerns were thoughts of teachers, classmates, and new friends. I was making my first attempt at learning a foreign language and had chosen Spanish.

Spanish class was only a short stroll down the hall from my homeroom, so I was one of the first to arrive. I took a seat at the back of the classroom so I could check out the others as they arrived. All the faces were new, but one in particular caught my eye. There was something about her. I noted how well her dark blue sweater contrasted with her brown hair. My eyes followed her as she took a seat close to mine.

Soon the teacher arrived and called the class to order. "I am Miss Santos," she informed us. She took a seat behind her desk. "As I call each of your names, please tell me something about yourself." She glanced at the list of students. "Barbara Andrews," she called, and looked out at the class. The girl who had caught my eye raised her hand.

"I'm a junior and assistant captain of the cheerleading squad," she said proudly in a musical voice.

I found it hard to concentrate on the others and kept glancing at Barbara and wondering what she was like. When my name was called, I raised my hand. Barbara looked around and our eyes met. All thoughts were driven from my mind. After what seemed like a long time, I managed to bring my thoughts under control. "I'm a sophomore," I stammered.

Miss Santos smiled. "I don't often have sophomores in my

classes," she said. "Why did you decide to take it this year?"

"I've wanted to study Spanish since I was in sixth grade, so I decided to take it as soon as I could," I answered. Miss Santos smiled again, then glanced down at her list.

I looked back at Barbara and found her smiling at me. I smiled back then looked away before anyone else could notice. My heart was beating faster. I wanted to sing! But I also felt confused. I had been told that feelings like these were what I would feel for a man. I quickly decided I should put Barbara out of my mind and not give her another thought.

Gym was my last class of the day, and I welcomed the break from academia. I was sitting on the last step of the bleachers watching the class assemble when Barbara walked in carrying her orange-and-blue pom-poms. She glanced about and saw me sitting there. She waved, smiled, and then made her way to the locker room.

A woman sitting next to me asked, "Do you know her?"

"She's in my Spanish class," I said, trying to sound casual.

"The cheerleaders practice during last hour," she said, answering my unspoken question.

Barbara would be in the locker room at the same time I was. That thought made the strange feelings return. I tried to shove thoughts of her aside, but I kept seeing her face in my mind.

As the term progressed, I found myself waiting impatiently for Spanish class so I could hear her voice as she recited. Then I couldn't wait for gym class. Occasionally, while dressing for gym, I would catch a glimpse of her bare shoulder just before she slipped into her cheerleader sweater, or see her dressed only in a bra and panties as she changed back into her street clothes. As I finished dressing, I would imagine caressing her and feeling her softness and warmth. I wanted to run my hands through her short brown hair and hear her speak my name. During this very turbulent and emotional time, I learned a name for what I was.

* * *

A new neighbor had moved in across the street. She wasn't like most of the women in the neighborhood. I watched her for a while, trying to figure her out. The neighborhood women wore dresses and were usually shepherding children. She always wore slacks, men's shirts, and work boots. She was often alone and seemed to keep to herself. I imagined she must be lonely.

One day I decided to go over and introduce myself. I felt a bit timid as I knocked on her door, not knowing how she would react to my being there. As I waited for her to answer, it occurred to me that maybe she liked being alone. As I thought of going back home, she came to the door. She opened it wide and stepped out onto the porch. I had to look up to meet her eyes and felt relief that they held welcome.

"I'm a neighbor," I said. "I live in the white house across the street."

She looked across the street and nodded. Her gaze turned back to me. "I'm Nora," she said, extending her hand.

"Marcie," I said as I shook it.

"Would you like to come in?" she asked.

I nodded.

She closed the door behind us. "Have a seat," she said, motioning toward the flowered couch. "Can I get you a soda?"

"Yes, ma'am. I'd like that," I answered.

As she walked toward her kitchen, I realized how ridiculous her large body would look in the kind of dresses the women in the neighborhood wore. Besides, she seemed comfortable dressing the way she did.

She returned with the soda, handed it to me, then seated herself in one of the chairs.

"Are you in high school? You look about that age," she said.

"I'm a sophomore," I replied, and took a drink of the soda.

She nodded. "I guess you'd like to know something about me," she said, half-amused.

"I admit I'm curious," I answered.

"I was a nurse during the Korean War, and then chose to pursue a career in the army," she explained. "I retired recently and decided to come back home."

Momentarily there was a look in her eyes that I couldn't understand, but she continued her story before I could think about it.

"When I went to East Saint Louis Senior High, it was a small building downtown. Nothing like the nice school you go to."

We were quiet for a moment, then she said, "I'd like to show you something. I'll be right back."

She returned with what appeared to be a picture frame. She sat next to me on the couch.

"These are my sharpshooter medals," she said proudly. "That one," she said, pointing to a miniature rifle, "I won when I outshot every man on the field."

"Wow, are you still that good?" I asked.

"I got a five-point buck last winter," she boasted.

I didn't know what a five-point buck was, but she was proud of it. I smiled broadly.

"The other medals aren't very impressive," she said. She set them aside. "Now tell me about you." Her brown eyes showed genuine interest.

"I'm the fifth oldest of ten children, and the oldest one at home now. My interests range from reading and playing guitar to coaching a softball team. I like to play volleyball too."

Then she asked the question I dreaded most. "Do you have a boyfriend?"

"No," I answered honestly. "Most of the guys want to talk about cars, and frankly, I'm not interested."

To my surprise, she smiled, and nodded as if she had already figured I didn't.

Thoughts of Barbara came to mind, and I suddenly wanted to run, before she could know what I was thinking. I stood and said, "Nora, I have to go now and help Mom with dinner, but I'll be back."

Her eyes held mine with a measuring stare, but she didn't try to stop me.

"Come anytime. I've enjoyed our talk."

"Thanks for the soda," I said as she saw me to the door. I almost ran home. Somehow Nora seemed to know something about me, and I wasn't entirely comfortable with that thought.

I rushed into the house and found my mother in the kitchen. Standing in the doorway, I told her about Nora.

"Mom, I met our new neighbor. Her name is Nora. She's a retired army nurse and has sharpshooter medals too. Nora got a five-point buck last winter," I said in one breath.

Mother gave a look of warning and glanced in the direction of the living room.

In my enthusiasm to share my information about Nora, I had rushed by without seeing my father.

He made a disapproving sound and rustled the newspaper. "Hunting is not for women," he said gruffly. "The mannish bitch ought to get herself a husband." The newspaper rustled again.

I turned to make a comment and felt my mother's restraining grip on my arm. "Will you peel the potatoes?" she asked gently.

Before I had the chance to talk with Nora again, I discovered something about her. Nora had a lady friend. At least once a week her bright green Chevrolet was parked in front of Nora's house. My first impression of her was that she must be a professional of some sort, as she usually wore skirts and matching jackets.

I looked forward to seeing Nora after her friend had visited. She always seemed to be so happy then. The sadness in her eyes, that I believed must have come from being a nurse in the Korean War, would be replaced with joy. We never spoke of the other woman, so I never learned her name or anything about her.

One evening when my father came home from work, I could tell by the noise he was making that he was in a bad mood. I wished in vain that I was upstairs safely in my bedroom, but unfortunately I was in the kitchen. I braced myself as he stormed into the room. He headed for the refrigerator and got a beer. He took a long swallow, then sighed. By the way he stood I knew he was mad about something. I glanced over at my mother. She was drying her hands on a towel. "Supper will be ready soon, dear. Why don't you read the paper while you wait," she said soothingly.

He took another drink, then crushed the can.

"You never see her with a man," he said. "And she's always dressed like one." His contempt was plain in the tone of his voice. "Mannish bitch."

I didn't have to ask who he meant, and Mother's silence seemed to indicate she knew as well.

"Every time you turn around, that blond bitch is over there. I wonder what those queer do in bed," he said contemptuously as he turned and left the kitchen.

"I'll be right back," I told my mother, and went upstairs to my room. My thoughts raced as I sat there hearing his words repeat in my mind. I wanted to talk to Nora. I wanted to know if she felt for the blond lady what I felt for Barbara.

At dinner my father was still in a sullen mood. I kept my eyes on my plate and desperately tried to avoid calling his attention to me. Just when I thought I'd get through dinner without a tirade, he dropped the bombshell. "Marcie, I don't want you to go over there," he said in a tone that indicated no argument was possible. "I don't want you near that queer again. Is that understood?"

I lifted my eyes to look at him as I answered. "Yes, sir." A look of hatred was in his eyes. I never visited Nora again, nor did I find anyone during high school to share my feelings with.

* * *

In college the game seemed to accept more diversity in its players, and amidst this freedom I found courage.

I met her in the fall of 1970, during my junior year at Southern Illinois University. I was in the cafeteria of the student union, struggling over the material for a quiz in geography.

Mary Lou flipped into the chair across from me. "Another map quiz?" she asked solicitously.

"Yeah," I said, and looked up. Next to Mary Lou sat a woman wrapped in a green cape. Her long blond hair cascaded over it. She leaned over the table and looked curiously at the map for a moment.

Mary Lou chose that moment to introduce us. "Louise, this is Marcie," she said, and we all turned quickly back to the map.

Louise was a whiz. She made sense out of squiggles that were rivers. Lakes, forests, and mountains were clearly visible to her eyes. I was impressed.

She was not what others would call beautiful. She was short and round, and had a square, heavy-featured face. But I saw a beauty and power in her that strongly attracted me.

We talked often after that and discovered our mutual love of music and sports. Her blue eyes would sparkle as we discussed the exploits of our favorite hockey player. That winter her parents took a ski vacation, and she invited me to stay with her while they were gone. The house sat apart from the others on the lane, at the edge of a forest. The tranquil setting soon worked its magic, and we began to relax.

Late one afternoon, after our classes, we came to the house. I put an album on the turntable as she prepared dinner. I built a fire and sat down in front of it. Shortly, she joined me.

"Dinner won't need my attention for a while," she said, making herself comfortable next to me.

I turned and our eyes met. At that moment I wanted to kiss her but was too shy to make a move. She sensed my desire and moved closer. Our lips met, our hands explored, and we made love. For both of us it was the first time with a woman. Our joy was so welcome yet so strange. It wasn't so much a conscious choice as it was a realization. It felt so right to love a woman, yet we felt guilt and shame for having tasted the forbidden fruit.

Even though we decided not to tell anyone, our actions spoke clearly. We spent every free moment together. Our happiness spilled out without conscious knowledge. Even though friends started acting strangely and conversation would cease when we entered a room, I knew I could not stop caring for her. I had taken the step and would never go back.

On Our Own

Under the Gaydar

Liz Morrison

"You know, I've brought out most of the lesbians on this campus," Peggy Coldon tells me with a big grin on her face. We're sitting in the Women's Space coffeehouse drinking herbal tea. I'm surrounded by posters of Billie Jean King, Angela Davis, Bella Abzug, and Cris Williamson. They look down at me as if they know something. I know Peggy wants to add me to her list of conquests, but as much as I'm questioning my sexuality I'm not ready to make that leap. At least not with her.

Peggy is a senior and head of the radical feminist-lesbian group on campus. She looks like a dyke with her messy short haircut and her uniform of Levi's jeans and a Levi's jacket. Although we're on a college campus and everyone wears that uniform, on Peggy it looks like a statement. She's a big woman, about 5-foot-10, with broad shoulders. From behind she looks like a man, but she doesn't care when she's mistaken for one. She knows who she is, and that's what equally attracts and repels me.

I'm 19 and very confused. Fact: I am attracted to women. Fact: I am attracted to men. I sleep with men, but I never seem to get emotionally involved with them. It's as if I've taken on the traditionally male role of enjoying sex for sex and not needing the reassurance of a relationship. Maybe I'm just a slut.

"Are you coming to the women's dance tonight?" Peggy winks at me as she says this. Her whole Don Juanita routine makes me feel creepy and flattered at the same time.

"Probably." I look up at her and see that she's trying to

be seductive by scraping the frosting from the top of her brownie with her index finger and slowly sucking it off. All this is doing is making me want a brownie.

Peggy gets up to leave. "Save me a dance tonight, OK?"

"I'll think about it."

I flirt with her because it makes me feel powerful.

Peggy's group of radical feminist-lesbians told me they've taken bets on which of them will have me first. The entire group totals five women, none of whom are appealing to me, and all of whom have slept with Peggy. I feel like a mail-order bride being sized up by the town before being sent off to marry someone I hardly know.

Women's dances at school are a combination of sexual energy, female bonding, and fear of being marked as gay. Lots of women—gay, straight, and bi—attend these dances just to be around other women. The dances are held in one of the cafeterias, and newspaper is taped up on the glass doors to give us privacy. Drunken fraternity boys stand outside the building and jeer at us as we enter and leave. They're threatened by women who don't want men. I actually like men, but I'm not sure if I still want to have sex with them. When they act like this, I find them repulsive.

"You need to meet the right man, honey. I got somethin' for ya right here."

"What are you girls, dykes?" They grab their crotches and lick their lips.

We glare at them and reply, "What are you, the alternative?" When I hear their comments I wonder if this is how I'll be treated if I come out as a lesbian.

I shake off this little incident and walk into the dance. Groups of women stand around watching the dancers and whispering. Some women are here to gawk; others, like me, are here to explore their feelings about their sexuality. The band, not surprisingly, consists of women and are all dressed in black leather jackets and jeans. I listen to the music for a moment and notice that the band has changed the "he" pronouns to "she" in each song. I wonder if anyone else notices this.

I've purposely come a little late in order to make an entrance. Looking across the room, I see Peggy and her entourage. Most of these women are still sleeping with her occasionally, and all of them are trying to get her attention, hoping to be chosen to go home with her tonight. I wave at them and they walk toward me. Each of them greets me with a hug and a kiss on the mouth. This is a step for me. Only recently did I allow another woman to kiss me on the mouth and then only as a greeting. Every chance they get, they tell me they're wearing me down and that it's just a matter of time before I break and sleep with one of them.

"You look pretty hot tonight," Judy says to me with a wink. I'm wearing exactly what they're all wearing: jeans, Frye boots, a turtleneck, and a jean jacket. Judy is Peggy's most recent ex. She's trying harder to be seductive because sleeping with me would really piss Peggy off. Dyke drama.

I dance to the fast songs, but I sit out all the slow ones. Many of my straight friends are here and I'm not ready to make a big statement, but I love the feeling of being sur-rounded by women. I look into the eyes of the woman I'm dancing with and openly flirt with her. I feel damp heat between my legs and a tingling sensation in my nipples. Suddenly every woman in the room is incredibly attractive to me. I need to have sex. With a woman. But I'm scared. I leave the dance feeling confused, my crotch throbbing and wet.

When I get back to my room, I call a guy I've dated a few times and ask him to come over. We have sex, but it turns into a wrestling match. I won't let him get on top. I want to do all the work, but he isn't quite that versatile. He doesn't understand that I'm using sex with men as practice, like a fact-finding mission. After he leaves, I fall asleep alone and unsatisfied.

I know I need to talk about these feelings with someone,

so when the semester ends and I go home for winter break, I'm really ready to see my closest childhood friend, Linda. She and I have known each other since we were 2 years old. Our parents and grandparents are all close friends, and we have a sisterly relationship that allows us to tell each other anything.

One night, at the home of another friend, she and I meet a few women we know from high school. All of us have returned from college and want to share our experiences. We play a sort of "Can you top this?" game with each other.

"I've slept with a woman," Joanie announces. We all look at her in stunned silence. Finally, my curiosity gets the better of me.

"What do you mean you slept with a woman? What, exactly, did you two do together?" I challenge her.

"Well, we took all of our clothes off, we kissed a lot, we touched each other everywhere, and we both came." She recites it like a checklist.

"Didn't you feel weird afterward?" Linda asks.

"Not at all. I felt like I was doing the most natural thing in the world."

Now I'm *very* curious and actually a little jealous. I have so many more questions, but I don't want to appear too interested.

"Would you do it again?"

"Are you kidding? I barely got out of bed to come home for vacation. I hardly studied for finals and I'll be lucky if I don't flunk out."

Everyone looks at her as if she's just been to a country we may never get a chance to visit.

In the car on the way home, Linda and I discuss what we heard.

"Do you think she made all that up?" I ask.

"She seemed to know what she was talking about." Linda looks at me, and we both start giggling. I feel relieved that the topic has finally been brought up between us, and I'm laughing because I'm nervous. I've wanted to bring this up with Linda for a while, but I'm afraid of losing her friendship. What if she thinks I'm attracted to her? That would be unlikely, given our long history as friends, but all of this is so new to me. I don't know any of the rules.

"Have you ever thought about sleeping with a woman?" I ask her.

"All the time," she replies. We drive in silence for a few minutes. I can't believe it. Not only is my best friend OK with me having these feelings, but she has them too. I can already hear my mother saying, "You're doing this because Linda is doing it." We used to dress alike as kids and copy everything the other one did. My mother will probably think this is a phase like when Linda and I just *had* to join the Girl Scouts. It didn't last long. I was thrown out and she quit.

"Do you think you're gay?" I ask her.

"I'm not sure. How about you?"

"I'm not sure either."

"You know I love you, but not in *that* way," I begin. Linda looks at me as if to say "Duh!"

"I'm so relieved I have you to talk to about this," she tells me.

"Yeah, me too. I was going crazy at school with all these feelings."

Linda pulls up in front of my house to drop me off. I open the door and step into the frozen night. The snow crunches under my boots as I walk up my driveway to the back door of the house. Instead of going in, I sit on the back step and look at the sky. There's no moon out tonight, but the stars are very bright so I decide to make a wish.

"Star light, star bright," I begin. This method of hope got me into my first-choice school, I tell myself. I close my eyes, repeat the wishing poem, and picture myself in an apartment in Boston with a bay window and a girlfriend. I open my eyes and realize I'm still a naïve 19-year-old college sophomore who can't decide which gender she's attracted to.

Linda calls me early the next morning. "Can you talk? I have to tell you something."

"Yeah, I'm here alone."

"I heard about a bar for lesbians from someone at school. I wanted to tell you last night, but I was too chicken. You wanna go tonight?"

"Are you sure it's a gay place?"

"I'm not completely sure, but let's check it out."

Later that evening Linda picks me up in her robin's-egg-blue Chevy Vega. It's the ugliest car on our street, but so far it's started every morning of this horrendous Buffalo winter without a jump.

"What's the name of this place?" I ask as I slide onto the blue plaid seat.

"Rosie's. It's somewhere down on Elmwood Avenue."

We drive for about 15 minutes and find the bar easily. I have a feeling that Linda's driven by here before but was too scared to go in alone.

"Have you ever been in this place?" I want to know if she's been holding out on me.

"No, but I've driven by it a bunch of times. I was afraid to go in by myself."

We park the car and walk up to the door. I try to be nonchalant as I attempt to look in the front window, but the bar name is painted in large swirling letters and obstructs my view. Linda and I look at each other as we walk through the door, feeling like two kids sneaking into the movies.

I'm not sure what I was expecting. The place is narrow and has long, rectangular tables lined up in rows like church pews along one side of the room. A bar runs the length of the other side of the room. The tables are filled with women wearing warm-up jackets. It looks like we've walked into a room of gym teachers. I'm so nervous that I ignore the obvious clues placed in front of me like street signs. The crowd is almost all women.

"Do you think this is really a gay bar?" I ask Linda.

"I can't tell. Let's get drinks and find someplace to sit."

The bartender is a short woman with a pile of curly hair. She looks at us suspiciously. We've both been legal for a year, so I don't know what her problem could be.

"Lemme see some ID," she barks. We produce our IDs and wait for her to inspect them. She tosses them back at us and asks what we want. Because I'm going through all these changes, I've started drinking weird drinks. I want to appear interesting, bohemian, sophisticated, and maybe even gay. I order a Campari and soda; Linda orders a beer. The bartender looks at me and snickers. I obviously don't look that intriguing to her. I take a sip of my drink and wince at its bitter taste.

We find a couple of seats and watch the people around us to find some sort of evidence that we're really in a gay bar. A few men are scattered among the women. No one looks particularly gay, and no one is kissing or holding hands. Some of the women look over at us and then begin whispering and smiling. The jukebox is playing "Shame" by Evelyn Champagne King, the same kind of music we listen to in bars at school. There are no show tunes or Judy Garland songs, no woeful women singing dreamy folk songs. Every time I make eye contact with one of the women sitting near us, I look away. I feel like they know we're impostors.

Linda gets up to use the bathroom, and I continue scrutinizing the crowd for gay clues. People are tapping their feet to the music or are engaged in deep conversations. This could happen anywhere.

Linda comes back from the bathroom, grabs my arm, and sits down next to me. "Oh, God! You are not going to believe this! I saw two girls kissing in the bathroom!"

Paydirt. The holy grail.

When I return to school for spring semester, I continue to think about all these new feelings. This thought process carries over into all of my junior year and the first part of my senior year, when I find myself involved in a relationship with a man, the soccer team captain. I've never been one to make hasty decisions. Meanwhile, my phone bills to Linda are astronomical.

One night I go to a party thrown by the girlfriends of the guys on the soccer team. It's supposed to be a big bonding experience for all of us, but I'm only going to this party to make my boyfriend, Dave, happy. I haven't been paying much attention to him lately, and he wants me to meet some of his teammate's girlfriends so we can all start socializing.

I walk into the suite where the party is being held and all my worst fears are realized. The room is full of tall, blond, WASPy women with names like Polly and Muffin. They all speak with severe lockjaw and wear a lot of bright green. I get a beer and try to find an ally in the chartreuse minefield of Stepford wives.

Scanning the room for a place to land, I see a pair of green eyes that lock into mine like a honing device and I'm struck by my immediate reaction to this woman. The attraction is so strong that I feel compelled to walk over to her and make conversation. The music is loud, so I have to scream into her ear, and as I lean over to speak to her I'm very conscious of how close I am to her face. She gives off a vaguely citrusy scent.

"I feel like a fish out of water here," I tell her.

She leans over to respond, and I feel her lips barely graze the top of my ear. I feel a warm sensation between my legs.

"Funny you should say that. This is my suite, but I don't really hang out much with my suitemates. Hi, I'm Cassie." She turns to shake hands with me and looks right into my eyes. She's tall and lanky, with an athlete's body. Her curly brown hair is cut short, more sporty than dykey. Her eyes remind me of sea glass.

"Nice to meet you. I'm Liz."

"I know who you are. You go out with Dave Rowe, the soccer captain."

"Yeah, we're kind of dating, but it's not serious. I have

a lot on my plate before graduation, so I don't have that much free time."

"I used to date him before he started seeing you. He's a really nice guy." She looks at my face for a reaction and adds, "I didn't sleep with him."

"I don't think you missed much. Sex with men is overrated." As if on cue, we clink our beer bottles together in a toast and smile at each other.

That same weekend, I decide to break up with Dave because I no longer feel anything for him. I tell him I'm too preoccupied with finals and job hunting to date anyone right now. We both cry because we know we've lost something. I've lost the ability to lie about myself.

I start hanging out with Cassie and her friends Kate and Lisa. Kate and Lisa are in a relationship and are both very attractive in a tall, blond "I can pass for straight" way. For the past three years I've heard rumors about their being gay, and I've been very intrigued by their ability to be so out on such a small campus. Everyone seems to accept them because the idea of them together is not all that unappealing.

For the rest of the semester, the four of us are inseparable. I feel sexual energy from Cassie, but I'm not sure how to handle it. When I go home for spring break, I talk to her on the phone almost daily. We never discuss our attraction for each other.

When school starts again that April, I know I have to do something about my feelings. One day Cassie and I are having lunch alone in the cafeteria.

"There's something I have to tell you." I look at her and I feel like I'm going to be sick. Taking a deep breath, I let the words fall out of my mouth like loose teeth. "I'm attracted to you." There, I said it.

"I know. I feel it." She pauses for a moment and looks away. "I'm attracted to you too, but I'm also attracted to Kate. In fact, we kissed last night." This can't be happening. Kate's with Lisa! What's going on here?

"Aren't Kate and Lisa together?" I ask her.

"Yeah, but they sort of have an open relationship. Look, I don't mean to hurt your feelings, but I really want to sleep with Kate. I'm being honest with you."

I get up from the table, go back to my room, write in my journal until my hand is numb, then go into the bathroom and throw up.

But the dyke drama is short-lived. Kate treats Cassie like a one-night-stand and their friendship begins to falter.

One night Cassie comes over to study with me. My room is small, and the only place to spread out with all our books is on my bed. I had the forethought to buy a double mattress from the Salvation Army at the beginning of the year. The standard dorm-issue cot made the room feel like a nun's cell.

"You can have the bed and I can spread my stuff out on the floor," I tell her.

Suddenly I'm feeling awkward and shy. Having her in my room and on my bed is overwhelming. I'm sure she can see my heart pounding under my shirt. She looks at me and smiles. "I don't need the whole bed," she says.

I take this as an invitation and climb on to the end of the bed with my books. After I settle in, I calculate the number of inches between her leg and mine as I keep reading the same paragraph again and again. I find excuses to reach for things that are just beyond her, and I "accidentally" brush her leg with the back of my hand. She shifts positions so that her thigh is resting against mine. I can hardly breathe.

After an hour of switching positions and trying to study, Cassie decides to take a nap. She turns over on her side and faces away from me, with her ass resting against my leg. I continue reading the same paragraph. She burrows herself deeper into my thigh and her breathing becomes rhythmic. I want to hold up a white flag at this point. Having her body nestled against mine makes studying impossible. I put down my book in defeat and lie down beside her, my chest pressed against her back, my face buried in the nape of her neck.

Slowly I tangle my hand in her hair, massaging her scalp. I breathe in her citrus scent and imagine that the two of us are lying in a grove of orange trees. I close my eyes and picture myself slowly peeling the skin from a large, ripe orange and sucking the sweet juice from my fingers as I pull the fruit apart. As I imagine how the soft, fleshy orange slice would feel in my mouth, I open my eyes as Cassie turns over to kiss me. At first she's tentative, but I am too aroused to let her tease me, and I press my mouth on hers, engaging her in a long, deep kiss.

I close my eyes and we are back in the orange grove, feeding each other fat, ripe pieces of fruit. I bite into a piece and let the warm juice run down my chin and onto my chest. We're rolling on the ground, my mouth finding her sweetest parts; her fingers are inside me.

We make love until the middle of the next day. When Cassie gets up to tell me she needs to go back to her room and study, I feel a little relieved. I need to be alone with all these new feelings right now, and, of course, I need to call Linda.

Once Cassie leaves, I jump out of bed and run to the mirror, half expecting to see a big red "L" in the middle of my forehead. I scrutinize my face for any changes, for the big transformation, for some kind of sign. I see someone who has finally made a decision, someone who is finally off the fence and on the ground. Grounded. I grab the phone and jump back into bed.

Overlooking the Obvious

Lynn Kanter

When I was a young child in the 1950s, I thought that women and men always wore formal attire when they went out on a date, and that the man routinely carried the woman in his arms. The image I had was quite clear: the woman in a swirly silver gown and matching high heels, the man in a black tuxedo and white shirt, effortlessly lifting his date to spare her such mundane chores as walking from the car to the door.

I didn't understand that a "date" had anything to do with sex or romance. I didn't realize that a wide range of apparel was permissible. I only knew that I did not want to wear a swirly silver evening gown or be carried in some man's arms.

By the time I became a teenager and went out with boys myself, I had, of course, given up this strange concept of dating. But in that predawn of feminism, there were conventions more difficult to buck. One was the expectation that girls were to instantly discard the plans we had made with each other if the slightest chance arose to spend time with a boy— any boy. I could never get over the fact that this behavior was not only considered acceptable, but strongly encouraged. My inclination was exactly the opposite.

In fact, my inclination was the opposite of the norm in any number of ways. All my silver-screen crushes were on actresses. I developed intense attachments to my female friends. On streets and buses, I noticed only the women. My favorite movie was *The Children's Hour*.

You might think all of these idiosyncrasies would serve as

clues to my true nature. But to think that would be to disregard my lifelong talent for overlooking the obvious.

* * *

Her name was Amy. She lived one floor above me in the dorm of a women's college in upstate New York. Amy had blue eyes, small hands, long blond hair. She was 21, an age that at 19 I considered alluringly mature. She had lived her entire life in one tiny town, an achievement to someone like me, who had spent my teens moving with my family from state to state. She was bright, observant, energetic. Best of all, she was a marvelous storyteller.

Amy's life was full of small adventures, and she recounted each one with such color, verve, and freshness that the story seemed to unfold right there in her overfurnished dorm room. She acted out all the parts, creating vivid characters with the tiniest of details—the hitch of a shoulder, the tilt of a head, the flawless replication of an accent.

I found Amy endlessly entertaining, and started spending most of my evenings with her. At about 10:00, after I had finished studying, I would bolt upstairs to be greeted with a cup of thick, sugary coffee that Amy had made on her forbidden hot plate. We would tell each other stories and share the day's experiences, joined occasionally by friends drawn in by our laughter. Eventually the friends would drift, yawning, away, but Amy and I would chatter on, stopping only when interrupted by the cacophony of morning birds. Entire nights vanished without a trace. This happened over and over again.

I described the mystery of the disappearing nights to my friend Charlotte, a woman with the sallow skin, jutting jaw, and darkened teeth of advanced anorexia. Sitting up weakly in her bed, surrounded by pillows that could not protect her from her own sharp bones, Charlotte smiled knowingly and said, "Looks like you're on to something new."

I did not ask her what she meant, just as I didn't ask her why she couldn't eat or how serious her illness was. Her eyes closed wearily. After a few moments I turned out the light, closing her door softly behind me. Charlotte left school soon after that. I never saw her again.

Meanwhile, other mysteries were taking place in my life, mysteries I didn't share with my friends. I appeared to have lost both my ability and my need to sleep. Everything began to fascinate me: classes, cookware, a new book, a song I had heard hundreds of times before. My energy was inexhaustible, fueled by the nightly narrative marathons in Amy's room. And most baffling of all, my hormones appeared to be in an uproar. A sexual current was running through me all the time, for no apparent reason.

Very late one night, I set my empty cup on Amy's cluttered dresser and looked around for my shoes. "I'd better go," I told her, "before those damned birds start singing again."

"Why don't you stay?" she asked. "It's too late for you to be walking downstairs to your room."

I hesitated. This seemed plausible, though the commute would have taken about 30 seconds.

"Come on." Amy patted a spot beside her on the bed. "I won't touch you."

Of course she won't touch me, I thought as I removed my jeans but primly retained my T-shirt and underwear. What made her think I was worried about that? Why would she even say such a thing? Gingerly I lay down with my back toward her, teetering on the edge of her narrow dormitory cot.

Amy lied. She did touch me, and I touched her, all through what remained of the night. We didn't put a name to what we were doing; we didn't even acknowledge we were doing it. But we were making love, and it was the most thrilling experience I had ever known.

Seconds later, it seemed, the sun broke through the window blinds. Outside our door, rubber soles slapped down the hall toward the bathroom. Amy and I kissed goodbye, with barely enough time to shower and change for class.

I remember with perfect clarity the exultation that lifted me on that spring morning two decades ago, and the thought that sounded in my head as I floated down the stairs to my own room: *Thank God I'm not normal.*

What I meant was: Thank God I don't have to be ordinary. What I meant was: Thank God I'm safe from the staid suburban life for which I've been trained all these years. What I meant was: Thank God I finally know where I belong, and it's in a woman's arms.

I had almost—but not quite—come out to myself. In the easy, earnest ethos of the times, I believed that I was now free to love wherever my heart led me, whether that meant men or women. I did not yet think of myself as a lesbian.

The school I attended, Kirkland College, had been born in the 1960s and died in the '70s, shortly after I graduated. It was remarkable in many ways, one of them being that it was considered unremarkable for women to love women. Rita Mae Brown came to speak, and Alix Dobkin played a women-only concert in the student coffeehouse. I remember seeking advice from my favorite professor about whether I should stay with a man I was dating or drop him in favor of the woman I was also seeing. We had this debate in front of the man himself, by discussing an analogous passage in *Howard's End.*

So not until I left college and reached the "real world" of Chicago, where feminism was blowing through the city like the raw, powerful wind off the lake, did I realize that following my flighty heart was no longer enough. I had to face the fact that it was no coincidence that the people I fell in love with were women. I had to claim the name *lesbian,* with all the pride, power, and defiance that word implies. I had to choose sides. And when I did—swiftly, and with the gratitude of having found a home at last—*that* was my coming-out experience.

Or at least it was one of them. Like most lesbians, I've had many more.

There was the first time I came out to a friend, hesitantly doling out my words on the dark back porch of her parents' house, as Joni Mitchell's "Little Green" quavered from the radio. Sarah listened to me with perfect openness and generosity throughout that tumultuous summer. It was the season of Watergate, the month Richard Nixon resigned from office, but I was too distraught over the dissolution of my relationship with Amy to pay attention to the dissolution of that administration. Years later, I would let Sarah drift out of my life because she chose a way of life I could not accept, marrying into Orthodox Judaism, with its disrespect for women.

There was the time I came out to my parents, weighing the possibility that I might lose them against the certainty that I would lose them if I kept my true self a secret.

There was the time I came out to my grandmother, who told me she had known for years and wasn't it nice I had found such a lovely girl.

There was the time I came out to a friend from high school, a straight woman who agreed that the teenage intensity we had once felt for each other must have been love.

There was the time I told my boss, and the time I insisted she tell a job candidate she was interviewing so we'd have no homophobes in our department, and the time when National Coming Out Day rolled around and I couldn't think of another soul to tell.

Then there are the times I've forgotten to come out. My aunt was recently shocked to learn that I had broken up with my partner of 10 years—shocked because she hadn't realized that we were together. She had seen my partner at innumerable family events; she had been in our home with its two female occupants and its single bedroom. At what point should I have taken my aunt aside and said, "By the way, you *do* realize I'm a lesbian?" And yet, by mentioning my separation, I was not coming out; I was merely behaving like a person who believes her life's events are worthy of inclusion in the family tapestry.

Even now, after these years of practice, coming out is not always easy. I surprise myself sometimes by stumbling over the words. Occasionally I substitute the word *gay* for the more proud and precise *lesbian*. Still, I push myself to come out whenever it's appropriate and often when it's not: for my own sake and for the sake of women who have more to risk than I do.

My true coming-out story—like that of all lesbians—cannot be told in the past tense. We have yet to see how it ends.

Dreams of Friends and Lovers

Pandora Nu

Vanessa and I squealed like pubescent girls who'd just spotted their teen idol as we ran toward each other across the baggage claim area. You've probably been annoyed by people just like us at the airport. But if you knew the whole story behind what we'd been through, leading up to this moment, and what would happen to us, you might not judge us so harshly. You see, by the time the plane approached the D.C. area it was already three hours later than I'd planned to arrive. Then, to make matters worse, the de facto prison with wings circled around Dulles for an hour. After my first semester at McGill University, which had resembled an academic triathlon, I was teeming with the anticipation of seeing Vanessa.

When I got to Dorval International Airport at 3:00 P.M., I believed I'd be in D.C. in time for a late dinner and a night out on the town with Vanessa. But I should've known by noon that things wouldn't go as planned. The flurries had turned into snow that was heavy enough to convince me not to schlep my suitcase from my dorm to the bus stop. Fortunately, I caught a cab from downtown Montreal with Carrie, the only real friend I'd made at McGill. Although she was going to New York, we were taking the same Eastern flight to La Guardia. I took out my Walkman to pass the time. I searched my backpack for the Suzanne Vega tape and popped it in. It was cued to "Marlene on the Wall." The music put me in a semihypnotic state, bringing me back to my 17th birthday. On that sweltering summer night, Vanessa and I had snuck into the 9:30 Club in D.C. to see Suzanne Vega. As the risk taker, I'd convinced her to go. Back then, it was the only way I got to do anything other than go to school, go to work, or watch my younger siblings. Vanessa, however, had never been in the city without her parents—much less to a club that we would've never gotten into if they'd bothered to card us. It was the first time we'd been complicit in something (other than seeing R-rated movies) that we had to keep from her mother and my father. In the middle of "Knight Moves," I was brought back from my reverie by a tap on the shoulder.

"Whatcha listening to?" Carrie asked.

"I don't know if you've heard of her..." I began, offering the headphones to her, "...Suzanne Vega."

"Don't you want to listen to something more festive?" she asked, returning the headphones to me. "I mean, we made it through our first semester, and now we get to go home for Christmas. Personally, I can't wait to see Tommy. I thought I was going to die before today came. I actually considered dropping out of school two weeks ago."

"That music reminds me of Vanessa," I said.

Vanessa Alvarado had been my best friend—and more of a sister than either of my stepsisters—since the summer between my sophomore and junior years of high school. My sophomore year at Winston Churchill High School merely represented one less year until I would go to college, leaving my suburban purgatory behind. Vanessa was a grade below me. I'd first met her in Mrs. Montoya's honors Spanish class. Though she was Bolivian and spoke Spanish, she hadn't studied in Spanish since the age of 9, when her family had arrived in the U.S. under political asylum. She sat behind me in class, but I hadn't paid attention to her during the school year because, after all, she was a freshman. At the end of the year when she asked me to sign her yearbook, I wrote in microscopic print in the lower left-hand corner of the back page:

Rent *Dreamscape*.
It's currently my favorite movie.

Dennis Quaid is a babe.
Have a nice summer.
Pandora Nu

Two weeks later I was already sick of working at the mall. As I was heading into Roy Rogers, I ran into Vanessa.

"Hi, Pandora," Vanessa said, sounding genuinely glad to see me.

"Oh, hi, Vanessa," I said, glancing at the "I am Sears" name badge pinned to her blouse.

"Are you working at the mall too?" she asked meekly.

"Yep."

"Me too."

"I know," I said, directing my eyes toward the name badge.

"Oh, yeah," she said, blushing. "Where are you working?"

"B. Dalton."

"That's all the way on the other side of the mall."

"Yep."

We stood in silence for a minute. I heard my stomach make an unattractive noise. At that moment I decided that my roast beef sandwich was more important than being polite, so I started to walk around her and into the restaurant. She slid over in the direction in which I was passing her. I stopped short of stepping on her loafers.

"I rented *Dreamscape* last week," she said.

"That's nice," I said, increasingly annoyed. I took a pre-meditated step toward the entrance, brushing her shoulder as I walked by her.

She turned to follow me and said, "You were right. Dennis Quaid's really good looking...." I continued walking toward the line to place orders. "...and I thought the idea that we could work out our problems in our waking lives if we could understand the symbolic meanings of our dream lives was really interesting." I stopped so hard that the soles of my partially laced combat boots left skid marks.

"That's why I love that movie," I said, knowing I'd made a profound connection with a kindred soul. She jaunted up to where I was standing in line. "Hey, do you want to have lunch with me? I totally want to talk to you about that."

"I'd love to, but I can't," she said, checking her watch. "After all, 'I am Sears.'"

"I get off at 5. Wanna hook up after work?"

"I get off at 5 too, but my mother's picking me up. We're going to have dinner and go to mass."

"Mass? But it's Wednesday."

"We go to evening mass three times a week."

"What about the weekend?"

"Only on Sunday morning."

"Only on Sunday morning," I repeated, shaking my head. "No disrespect and all, but you Catholics may not believe in preventing unwanted pregnancy, but y'all sure seem to believe in preventing much-wanted fun." I was next up to order. Reaching into my black, non-designer jeans, I pulled out a pen and an old receipt. I wrote down my phone number and handed it to her. "Call me tonight," I said.

"Is 9:30 OK?"

"That's cool with me."

That night Vanessa called at precisely 9:30. We started out talking about the relationship between fear, the power of the subconscious to deny knowledge of the truth, and the mind's ability to sublimate that knowledge through dream symbolism. After the first hour, we digressed into a myriad of other topics: the abuse of power by government, be it democratic or autocratic; the pros and cons of scientific experimentation on humans; the cliché of the boy-meets-girl-who-doesn't-like-boy-but-they-end-up-together-in-the-end formula of Hollywood movies. As the night went on, Vanessa began to tire. She spoke in Spanish because it was more comfortable for her to think and talk in the same language. I understood this feeling because until I was 5 it was more comfortable for me to think and talk in Taiwanese. When I hung up, it was hard to believe that we'd talked until midnight.

When my junior year began, there was an unexpected buzz about the friendship Vanessa and I had developed over the summer. We'd become so associated with each other that we were known as "Pan and Van, the semi-Siamese twins." Our reputations made us unlikely friends. The previous year Van had been "the new girl," making her somewhat mysterious. She was "girly" in that she dressed in Benetton tops and Guess jeans and wore makeup. She was "ladylike" in that her speech was demure and proper.

I was perceived as anything but mysterious, girly, or ladylike. I'd moved to Potomac, Md., from Richmond, Va., during the summer before eighth grade. I learned quickly that my Southern accent caused people to assume I was slow and uneducated. To cover it up, I talked like I was a big-haired blond straight from the Valley. My image irked the smart kids in my classes, particularly the "model minority," first-generation Chinese students.

Since freshman year, my inner circle of friends was composed of the artsy, outsider clique. We called ourselves the Nomads because we were always on the move, always trying to elude societal labels and parental definitions. Perhaps the biggest reason I wasn't the typical math-geek, ABC (American-born Chinese) student was because of the way I dressed. I wore all black all the time, usually men's clothing. My look spurred rumors about my sexuality—especially because two of the Nomads, Blake and Jillian, had come out as bisexual and lesbian, respectively.

If the students at Churchill had looked more closely, they would've seen that Van and I had some fundamental physical traits in common. We both had straight black hair, fair skin, and a sprinkling of freckles. We both had extremely dark brown eyes that were less than round but more than almond-shaped.

If the students at Churchill had known us better, they would've understood that the thing that made us best friends was what we had in common emotionally: parents who believed in control more than caretaking. Of course, their forms of totalitarianism manifested differently. My father believed that by allowing me to interact with boys only as academic and athletic rivals, forbidding me to date until I graduated from college, and discouraging friendships with "unambitious" girls, he could turn me into the asexual, materially successful, first-born boy he'd always wanted. Van's mother believed that by going to mass four times a week and keeping her ignorant about sex, she could turn Vanessa into a good Catholic girl who would marry a good Catholic boy who'd take care of her and their multiple children. But there was one salient difference between them as parents: Van's mother loved me like a daughter; my father loved no one, especially his daughter.

* * *

When Van and I reached each other at the airport, we embraced, screaming "¡Chiquita!" over and over. We jumped up and down, kissed each other on the cheeks, and hugged again. By the time we returned to the baggage carousel, the other passengers had gone and my suitcase was on the floor with the unclaimed bags. Van took my backpack and I towed my suitcase as we headed for the parking lot. Her tan Rabbit started right up. Van turned the heater up full-blast. Within minutes we were driving on the beltway in a car that was on the verge of going nova.

"I'm so glad you got my messages, *chiquita*," I said.

"You kept calling me when I was out for like five minutes to run an errand for *Mamita*." She took the exit toward the city. "I was beginning to get paranoid. I thought you were trying to avoid me."

"That's so funny. I thought you were trying to avoid me."

"After your second message, I was afraid you were going to call again and say you weren't coming back."

"*Loca,* how could you be so silly?" I laughed.

"Well, your letters made Montreal sound so good I was afraid you didn't want to come home."

"Montreal's great, but there are two reasons I never even considered not coming home: above-freezing weather, and you—not necessarily in that order."

"*Bueno,* now that you're here let's just be happy we're together," Van said. "So, where do you want to go, *chiquita*?"

"It's already midnight. I can't believe *Mamita* even let you pick me up," I said, noticing a sneaky grin form on her face.

"Before I even knew your flight was going to be delayed, I pretended that your father called and said I should spend the night at your house. She doesn't expect me home until dinner tomorrow," she said with pride. "Oh, by the way, *Mamita* invited you over for dinner."

"I'm glad to see my bad influence hasn't worn off yet," I said. "Let's go to Mr. Smith's. I feel like having one of their famous blueberry daiquiris."

"Too bad the drinking age in D.C. isn't like Montreal's. Reagan totally screwed things up for us. I hope they won't card on a Wednesday night."

While we drove, Van and I caught up on what was going on at Churchill and how things were with her mother, father, and brother. I told her about my torturous exams and how Carrie and I had gone to this club called Thunderdome to celebrate when we'd finished.

As usual, I barely mentioned my family. It seemed as though Vanessa and I had never been apart. We got to Georgetown before anxiety had time to supplant the joy of being "Pan and Van, the semi-Siamese twins" again.

Mr. Smith's Saloon was a ghost town. We sat at a table for two in a dimly lit corner. I was working on a blueberry daiquiri, and Van was sipping a Long Island iced tea. I'd just finished telling her a story about the time I faked a seizure so that my friends and I wouldn't have to wait in line to get out of a building. Van was laughing so hard that she snorted. I realized how far she'd come from her "That's so unladylike!" days. I was feeling so content that I was ready for the evening to end right then. Last call was less than an hour away anyway.

Between snorts Van asked, "So, when are you going to see Jonah?"

Before I could answer her, I swallowed my daiquiri the wrong way and coughed so violently that I thought I was choking to death. I went to the bar and returned with a glass of water. I took a couple of sips. "Oh, well, I might see Jonah at the hospital when I go to visit my ex-boss, but I don't think I'll be seeing much of him," I said, taking a sip of water before continuing. "The thing is, I broke up with him in October." Van just stared. "You see, I met someone up at school, and I didn't think it would be fair to him if I didn't break it off as soon as I knew I wanted to be with someone else."

"Well, that's good, *chiquita*," she said in a supportive tone. "You know how I feel about cheating. So, this new guy's got to be impressive if he can beat a third-year med student from a rich Long Island family who looks like he could be on the cover of *GQ*. I mean, if you hadn't already dated him I'd go out with him in a sec."

"Actually, you'll get to meet Simone the day after Christmas," I said meekly.

"*See-moan*," she said with a fake French accent. "How cool that you're dating a French-Canadian guy. That's such a better name than guys named *Mee-shell*. At least Simone doesn't sound like it's a girl's name."

I took another sip of water. I looked directly into Van's eyes. I inhaled deeply and exhaled slowly. "Well, that's the other thing. Simone is French-Canadian...and a girl."

Van started laughing. She laughed and laughed until her eyes rolled back in her head. She laughed until she was hyper-ventilating.

I remained in my chair, motionless, speechless, fearless. Convinced more than ever that if my friendship with Van was going to survive she would have to accept the truth, I stated firmly, "My French-Canadian girlfriend, Simone, is coming to visit the day after Christmas. She's going to stay until the day after New Year's, which is when I'm going back to Montreal too. I hope that you'll want to meet her."

Van stopped laughing. She stopped hyperventilating. She stopped making any sounds at all. She polished off the rest of her Long Island and went to the bar. She came back with a Long Island in each hand. As soon as she sat down, she knocked back the one in her right hand. She was about to pick up the one in her left hand when I caught her wrist. She recoiled as though she'd been grabbed by an assailant. The drink spilled all over her lap, causing her to jump out of her chair and run to the bathroom. I cleaned up the table and her chair. I bought her another drink and waited for her to return. Five minutes seemed like forever. When she came back to the table, she had a drink in her hand. She saw the one I'd bought on the table and pushed it toward me.

"You didn't have to do that."

"I don't mind. I feel bad that I spilled your drink." I pushed the drink back toward her.

"No, really, it's OK." She pushed the drink back so hard that it sloshed over the rim.

"Look, I bought it for you." I sent the drink back her way. "Drink it or don't drink it. I don't care. Besides, I don't think this is about the drink."

Van downed the one she'd bought for herself. Then she started crying. She folded her arms on the table and put her head down. I patted the top of her head, stroking her black hair, pulling loose strands behind her ears. Through the whimpers, I heard Van say, *"Si eres contenta, chiquita. Si eres contenta..."*

I leaned over and whispered in her ear, "I'm very happy, *chiquita,* but I'd be even happier if you were OK with this." Lifting her head and wiping the tears from her face, she said, "I'm not OK with it at this moment, but I'm sure I will be in the morning. For now, it would help me if you told me more about Simone."

I told her about how Simone and I had met in our survey of art history class. I told her about Simone's beautiful curly red hair. I told her about Simone's mother, who was a writer, and her father, who was an architect. I told Van that I'd told Simone all about her and that Simone was eager to meet her. I told her everything I could think of about Simone until it was time for Mr. Smith's to close. Then I got Van's keys and drove us back to Potomac.

By the time we got to my parents' house the Long Islands had kicked in. I opened the passenger-side door and helped Van out of the car. The trip from the car into the house and up the stairs was noisier than I would've liked. I was grateful that my father wasn't in the kitchen waiting for me, as was his custom. I'd taken off Van's shoes in the laundry room, so when we got to my room I plopped her on my queen-size bed and pulled the covers over her. Before I got to my side of the bed, I heard her snoring. Having left my bags in the car, I got under the covers in my clothes and promptly fell asleep.

That night I had a dream that Van came to the airport with me to meet Simone, and that we all ran to each other, howling with joy, embracing lovingly. When I woke up at 10 in the morning, Van was still asleep, so I went to the kitchen to get a couple of glasses of water to rehydrate her. By the time I returned, Van had awakened and was sitting up in bed. She smiled as I entered the room with the water.

"I'm so glad you brought water," she said, reaching for a glass. "I'm dying of thirst and I have a killer headache."

"That doesn't surprise me." I put the other glass on the nightstand. I went back to my side of the bed and snuggled under the covers. "But I am surprised you're up already. I mean, you really tied one on last night."

"Yeah, I must've." She took a large gulp of water. "But I couldn't sleep anymore. I had a really disturbing dream. I dreamed that you told me that you broke up with Jonah so you could be with a girl."

I pulled the covers over my head. I knew I wouldn't be able to hide the hurt from her. Actually, I think I really just wanted to hide.

Even though I was able to refresh her memory later that day and we remained best friends, things were never the same. Even though Van met Simone and treated her with respect and she asked us to come to her house for dinner and introduced Simone to *Mamita* as my girlfriend, and she said she felt bad for me when we broke up, a little part of me never came out from under the covers that morning. The little part that stayed under the covers was a part of me that was heart-broken because until that day I think I was also a little in love with her.

Coming Out: The Ripple Effect

Mary Vermillion

Magic Johnson is on TV at my second-favorite bar, announcing that he's HIV-positive. I admire his courage, so I tell my best friend that I think I might be a lesbian and that I'm obsessed with a woman on our volleyball team. She turns bright red and takes a long swig of Guinness. Things are changing too fast for her. Her brother was killed in a car accident a year ago, and since then we've spent almost every evening together. She is losing her haven, the apartment I share with my husband.

An old college friend visits and gives me a massage that can only be construed as sexual. I say that I am for sure bi— maybe lesbian. The backrub stops. I have misinterpreted her intentions. She is not like that. She had resigned herself to being homosexual, but then a minister laid his hands on her and drove it out. I ask if she is attracted to men. *Yes.* Any particular ones? Well, no, not actually. A week later she sends me a book called *Healing the Homosexual*. I send it back with a note saying "I hope you find what makes you happy."

I tell a woman on my volleyball team that I'm attracted to her. She's flattered, but nothing happens. Then, months later, she downs several shots of whiskey and makes love to me. She says it doesn't mean I'm a lesbian. I decide it does, and I leave my husband. A year and a half later, I leave her.

I mail a blurb to my 10-year high school reunion: *I'm*

getting divorced and finding new ways to love. When I call a friend to share my cryptic brilliance, she says it sounds like I've found Jesus.

My sister isn't surprised. "I was wondering," she says, "because you have so many gay friends. Are you going to tell Mom and Dad?"

A college friend tells me she French-kissed a woman once. They were both really drunk, of course, and it was just that one time.

I call a friend from high school to ask if he's coming to the retirement party for our former debate coach. He says no and asks how my husband is. I tell him we got divorced and that I married someone else. He politely asks for a name. Beth, I say, hoping he won't freak out. "Go, girl!" he whoops. He tells me he and David are celebrating their second anniversary. They own a house together, and their gladiolas are the envy of the neighborhood. We laugh, and he makes me guess who else is "riding the bus." His younger sister. We speculate about other people from our past, shrieking at each name.

A friend congratulates me on fulfilling myself. She gleefully tells me that her husband is threatened by her career.

My old study buddy from Chaucer class says she was in a threesome once with a man and another woman. She sips her wine and looks at me expectantly.

I run into a woman I haven't seen in years. I'm wearing a Pride Fest T-shirt, so I give her the condensed version: big changes, love my job, love my life with Beth. She honors me with a fuller narrative: She's gotten divorced. Since then she has bought and sold two houses. She's much better at buying houses and cars than her husband ever was. She became a grandmother, explored Ireland, and attended Clinton's inauguration. She quit her job as a secretary and became a union organizer.

I worry how my students will react, but this one begins talking about herself. She says that she was a surrogate mother. Nobody understands that it was one of the best times of her life. She and her 6-year-old son got to live in New York. They were treated royally, and she became extremely close with the couple—especially the woman, who sends her a picture of the little girl every Christmas.

My dad drives three-and-a-half hours to listen to me. *When did you know? Are you with someone? Can you keep your teaching job?* There is love and caring behind each question. He reminds me that he was in the Korean War. He never killed anyone, he explains, but he taught people to. He was an artillery trainer. When he left there, it was the best day of his life. What he doesn't say: He knows I have struggled to tell the truth about myself, and he wants to do the same.

Crush

Jenn Just

Last week I came across some memorabilia while I was cleaning my apartment. Among the papers and yearbooks was a copy of Wisconsin's queer newspaper. On the front page was a photograph of me with a group of women marching in Milwaukee's pride parade in the early 1990s. As I look at that picture and think about my crush, I can still feel that stir of confusion, excitement, and embarrassment flash through me.

* * *

My longest-lasting crush began in a women's studies class at the University of Wisconsin. Michelle. I was just coming out, and I was very tender and new. I'm not sure if I noticed her or her friend first; they were often whispering or making impressive statements in class while I sat back trying to blend in. She was definitely a dyke, and her confidence and audacity awakened me.

My relationships with female friends have always been intense, but in high school I moved from group to group, fearing rejection. I never really thought about my girl-friends in a sexual manner, although I did have to fight off jealousy when they went off with boys, leaving me uncomfortably stranded with the leftover dudes, most of whom creeped me out.

After high school, I ended up attending a small state university, because my "supportive" guidance counselor didn't think I could get into any top-level facility of higher learning. What a confidence builder!

During my freshman year at the university, I somehow became more attractive to men, which inflated my ego in a way I had never felt before. My sexual self began to emerge, and I loved the desire, sensuality, and power that came with my new sexuality. My girlfriends and I went to parties, and before we had too much to drink we'd pick out the guy that we wanted to get with at the end of the bash. The one who hooked up first always won free drinks or admission to the next party.

Sophomore year, I began my first serious relationship with a man. He was a virgin, so I got to teach him how I liked it. The sex happened quickly and often, but after a year together at school, and a few months living together in his home state, Kentucky, I knew he could never give me the affection and emotional support I craved. I bailed one night and got on a Greyhound headed toward the University of Wisconsin—the real thing this time—at Madison: a bigger, and liberal, more challenging place for me.

* * *

It's funny how unaware I was about my behavior. It seemed obvious to others, but not to me. When I was with boyfriends I had been attracted to their friends' girlfriends, but being a lesbian never crossed my mind. I was ardently close to my female friends, had mostly friendships with guys, and even had *lesbian neighbors* as I was growing up, so it wasn't that I was ignorant—I just didn't think of it. My lesbian neighbors were often talked about in negative ways or rarely mentioned at all, but they did pique my curiosity. Several people would tell me I was "in the family" before I would tell myself and I claimed the epitaph "dyke" as my trophy.

* * *

And then the women's studies course. The two of them whispered by the window across the room from me. I thought for certain she knew I was interested. Whenever she looked at me I became hot and flustered and couldn't stop smiling.

One day she walked into the deli where I worked. *Oh, my God,* I thought. My heart started pounding. Again I couldn't stop smiling. I couldn't stand still. I was so embarrassed about being seen there—*and* I was a vegetarian—what would she think to see me working among these meats! Of course this was one of the few times that I was covering the register. I wanted to disappear into the walk-in refrigerator, because what I really wanted to do was kiss her. I feared that my coworkers, who had no idea I was a dyke, would figure it out by my unusually hyperactive behavior and tell my macho boss, who would then fire me. And I really *needed* this job.

I ran behind the deli counter and tried to pull my supervisor away from the job she was doing, but with no luck. I flew over to where a coworker was stocking the refrigerator case and begged her to ring up this next customer, but she too failed me.

Oh, no, I'm going to start crying, I thought.

But I didn't have time for that, Michelle was waiting, and I was the only one to check her out. I cut behind the deli case and threw a joke to my supervisor, only to have it fall flat as I edged my way to the checkout. My mood shifted; my fear was making me sweat. *How sexy,* I thought gloomily as I wiped my brow, hoping I wouldn't drip on her.

So I just grinned foolishly while I checked her out. I took her money and barely breathed—I had never been so close to her. I was sure she could smell the stale, meaty odor that hung in my hair and on my clothes and skin no matter how many times I washed up. We said "hey" and figured out that we were in the same women's studies class. I don't really remember anything else except that we couldn't stop smiling at each other. My excitement heightened as I wondered if she was attracted to me or if she was just embarrassed because it was so obvious that I was crushed-out on her.

✷ ✷ ✷

While at the UW, I volunteered at an AIDS organization and was on the speaker's bureau. I felt like it was a respectable thing for me to do—go out into the world and talk about safe sex and hand out condoms and dental dams and such. Being on the bureau was more upbeat than my work as an emotional support "buddy," which I'd been doing for some time. I was the person who dressed up as a giant condom and walked in parades and went along with the speakers to high schools and fairs. I was the gimmick that hopefully people remembered before they had sex.

This was when the picture was taken. As I was happily marching and perspiring in that heavy condom costume in Milwaukee's gay pride parade—my first gay pride parade— out of the blue I thought: *What if Michelle is here? Would she come to Milwaukee for this? What if she sees me dressed like this? Will she think I'm straight or a fag hag?* I definitely didn't feel like I was coming out in that costume—rather, I was still hiding. I struggled for breath and made myself keep walking, waving, and throwing condoms to the crowd as their shouts infiltrated my mind's ramblings. "It's a dick." "Hey, Peter." "What a huge schlong." People were laughing and hooting, and I was just going along with it when I started to think about my role as the penis part of the costume. I had just been enjoying it before that point. How into this costume was I? Was I identifying with my male, "butch" side? I fretted over it. I didn't want to be seen as one or the other. I didn't want to be stuck with a label, especially because I was newly out and I already had one label to show for it, but I also didn't want to narrow my prospects. I was attracted to butch dykes as well as femme and androgynous women.

As the parade turned a corner I glimpsed a group of women passing me on the right. And who was among this group of hot and trendy dykes? Michelle. Instantly, I felt small and alone. I stopped waving to the crowd and throwing condoms. I stopped laughing; I slowed down my pace. I didn't know many of the lesbians from this hip crowd. How was I going to get out of the costume without them seeing me?

Then I recognized another classmate in the crowd. I boldly ran right into her and started talking too much. For once something good happened: I was invited to lunch with this amazing group of dykes. I hardly talked to Michelle, but her friends were smart, witty, and beautiful, and somehow I joined right in.

* * *

After moving all the way to San Francisco I ran into Michelle practically on my doorstep. Coincidentally, a friend from Madison was visiting, and he wanted a cup of coffee. We ran across the street to the Bearded Lady and we were chatting when suddenly, Michelle was right there. In a fluster I said hi, mumbled something, and ran out before I said or did anything embarrassing. *Too late!* I realized after I slammed the door. She could still get me flustered. Did she live in San Francisco or was she just visiting? What if she lived nearby? What would I—could I—do?

Throughout the eight years that I have since lived in the Bay Area I have run into Michelle—or, rather, Tom, as he now calls himself—many times. I'm not sure if he's had a sex change or how he identifies himself, but he still intrigues me. Usually we just say hi. Once I somehow got the guts— probably because I had a long-term girlfriend—to tell him about a construction job I had heard about. Would he be interested? I hoped to establish a rapport with him. I imagined that he was attracted to me and we would start hanging out. But nothing ever did happen. The gig didn't work out and he never returned my calls. At least I'll never regret not trying to talk to him.

Around that same time I began to question my sexuality again... Was I really attracted to Michelle, the woman? What did it mean if I was also attracted to Tom, the man? Was I just displacing my lesbian feelings onto Tom, or was I bisexual? And what was up with my girlfriend, who had recently become very interested in transgender and transsexuality issues and who now identified as a tougher, more male butch than when we had first got together? Wasn't I a big dyke? Why these attractions to women who identified and looked like men?

Most of the women I've gone out with were androgynous or butch-leaning, although the pretty ladies hold my interest from time to time. I began to pay more attention to who I was attracted to, to what sparked me sexually, and to how I reacted in different situations. I slept with all sorts of babes—younger, older, bigger, smaller, with many different skin tones, backgrounds, politics, and religions. Men are attractive to me, but I never really feel comfortable with them unless we're good friends, and even then the attraction doesn't have staying power. I'd had both amazingly good sex with some men and amazingly bad sex with other men. The same is true with women.

But sex wasn't really the reason that I came out as a dyke. I liked the fact that these butch women I was attracted to were really good at taking care of themselves. Most of the women I'm attracted to have this power and energy, and they can do anything as well as—if not better than—men, and I find that wonderfully beautiful. I've become more familiar with my own butch side, and I began to let go of my more feminine characteristics. Yet at times, I grow my hair out and don my more "girly" gear. It is tough to have a fluid identity and to fit into any one of the pockets of any community, and in the Bay Area I have found it particularly difficult to meet new women, since my image changes often.

Last summer I ran into Tom again. We run into each other once or twice a year…usually at the queer film festival. We don't talk much, but we usually acknowledge each other. I'm still a bit nervous and try to act cool. He just is. This innocent crush reminds me of my early years as a dyke, and I value the energy and interest that arises in me when I run into him. My longest dyke crush. What could be better?

* * *

So, back to the newspaper: The photo on the cover of the paper shows a large *condom* in a parade, waving at the crowd. Michelle and her friends are trailing slightly behind me. The anxiety, embarrassment, and delight of that moment still warm my heart. But at least in that Kodak moment, safely ensconced in that silly costume, I knew I had discovered something new inside me, an intensity that would change me in ways I couldn't predict. I was on a journey to a new way of being, and my heart was wide open.

The Summer of '83

Lesléa Newman

It was real hot that summer, the summer of 1983. I spent most of my days lying naked on my bed, reading Ann Bannon's Beebo Brinker books. That certainly didn't do anything to cool me down. I had just come out two months before, and I wanted a lover more than I had ever wanted anything in my whole life. I'd been straight for 27 years, and I knew there was something wrong the whole time. My mistake was that I thought there was something wrong with me. Why didn't I like being with men? Why would I rather go to the movies, go bowling, go to a natural history museum, go anywhere but to bed with them? I had a problem. I always thought that I was with the wrong man, but the *real* problem was that I was with the wrong sex.

So I moved to Northampton, Mass., in December 1982, where there were more dykes per city block than anywhere else in the world, or in New England at least. Within a few months, I was *out*—I cut my hair, threw away my brassieres, bought a pair of Birkenstocks, and moved out of my coed cooperative house into an apartment with Anita, a dyke of four or five years. In short, I had done everything but *it*, the big *it* that I had only read about in every piece of lesbian literature I could find. I felt like a teenager again, when I was the last virgin on the block. When, oh, when, would I ever find a lover?

Anita didn't have a lover either that summer, so we spent a lot of time together kvetching, shvitzing, and comparing crushes. One day, after reading a particularly juicy scene from *Odd Girl Out*, I announced to Anita that we had to go dancing that weekend at the Girl's Club, a women's bar a few towns away. Neither of us had ever been there before, and somehow that made it safer and scarier than a dance in our own community. I was determined to go to that bar and bring a woman home with me. After all, it was August already, and if the whole summer passed without me kissing a woman I knew I would just die.

Anita agreed to go Saturday night. To make things even more exciting, she came up with a bet: Whoever was first to ask a woman she didn't know to dance would get her laundry done by the loser for a month. Wow. Stakes were high. I sure didn't want to be schlepping Anita's smelly T-shirts and shorts to the Laundromat for a whole month. But just the thought of asking a woman I didn't know to dance made my knees buckle. "Ask someone you don't think is cute," Anita said. "Then it's not such a big risk, and it won't matter so much if she says no." But what good was that? I didn't want to dance with someone I didn't think was cute. And besides, the possibility of someone saying no hadn't even occurred to me. You mean that once I got up my nerve to ask, she could refuse? Now I was even more apprehensive.

Saturday night rolled around, and Anita and I spent about two hours trying on everything we owned before coming up with perfect outfits: She wore light-blue jeans and a black muscle shirt; I wore white pants and a red low-cut top. I bought all kinds of buttons, which we laughingly pinned on each other: SO MANY WOMEN, SO LITTLE NERVE; SOME DO, SOME DON'T, I MIGHT; and START YOUR DAY WITH ME. Of course, as soon as we got to the bar we took the buttons off and hid them in the glove compartment of Anita's car.

The bar was crowded and smoky. To escape the heat, a lot of women were standing around out in the parking lot, including a whole softball team in uniform. I felt really shy walking past all these women, who laughed and talked and stood so easily together, some leaning against the parked cars with their hips touching, drinking beers and looking up at the sky. Anita led me inside, and we sat down at a little table, listening to the music and watching the women who were dancing. Then we danced together a few times, which was fun but not exactly what I had come for. *Hell,* I thought, *if I wanted to dance with Anita all night, we could have just stayed home and played Michael Jackson records on the stereo.* When a slow song came on, I told Anita I was going to sit at the bar, and she made a motion to follow me. I shook my head. "Anita," I said, "no offense or anything, but if we dance one more dance together, everyone will think we're an old married couple. You go back to our table and I'll go sit at the bar." I looked at my watch. "Let's rendezvous in an hour, OK?" She nodded and left me to meander over to the bar alone.

I sat on a stool with my elbows leaning back on the bar and watched the dancers for a while. A fast song was on now, and I loved watching all those sweaty bodies moving—hips swaying, breasts bouncing up and down, tuchuses shaking. *Sigh.* I let my glance wander among the tables lining the dance floor until it landed on a dark-haired woman sitting alone, smoking a cigarette and nursing a beer.

That was *her.* Something in me just knew it. I studied her closely. She was sitting low in her chair, with her arm flung carelessly across the table and her legs up on the empty chair across from her. She wore a white button-down shirt and tight black pants. No buttons, no jewelry. She was suave, cool, tough, detached. I didn't know the word *butch* yet, but I knew I liked what I saw.

I continued to watch her for a while, wondering just how I would approach such a woman. Soon her head turned slightly and she looked in my direction. My stomach practically fell to my feet, the way it sometimes does when I ride an elevator, but I held her gaze. A flicker of a smile crossed her face before she turned away. And before I could move she turned back. This time I smiled.

Why had she looked my way? I'd like to think she could feel my stare burning a hole in her cheek, though later Anita pointed out that the clock was hanging on the wall above the bar right behind me. I guess it doesn't really matter why she looked at me. I was just glad she did, which I guess was obvious, because eventually she came over and asked me to dance. I thought for sure she was getting up to leave, or to go to the bathroom or something, but she very slowly and calmly walked up to the bar, stood right in front of me, and said, "Wanna dance?" Just like that.

I nodded and slipped off my stool. She took my hand and led me onto the dance floor. *Oh, my God, she's holding my hand,* I thought as we passed Anita, who was still sitting alone at our table.

We danced two dances together without saying a thing, and then what I was dreading and hoping for happened: A slow song came on. She (I still didn't know her name) opened her arms, and I gracefully fell into them.

We danced through that song and the next slow one, and let me tell you, she was some dancer. She had both her arms tightly around me and one leg planted firmly between my thighs, rotating in a manner that was driving me wild. And if that wasn't enough, she started planting little kisses down my neck and across my collarbone, which was peeking out of my shirt. I closed my eyes in sheer ecstasy, hoping that Brooke Shields would never stop singing about her "precious love." At one point I looked up and caught sight of Anita still sitting by herself and watching me dance, her eyes practically popping out of her head. I closed my eyes again, letting my body sway and time stand still until the song was over.

After two more fast songs, Mary (I had finally asked her name) asked me if I wanted to get some air. I did, and as we walked out to the parking lot, she took my hand again. I followed her past parked cars with women leaning against them, past some trees, past the lights of the street, toward a darkened corner of a field with a baseball diamond in it. At that point, I would have followed her anywhere.

She leaned back against the metal fence and pulled me close to her. Finally. Thank God, I thought, as her lips met mine. All the reading I'd done, and all the fantasizing, hadn't prepared me for the softness and the strength and the rightness of that first kiss. I felt like my whole body was rushing toward my mouth, crying *More, more!* I got weak in the knees and wet in the pants. My mouth sought hers again and again. "God, you're beautiful," she said, stopping for air, and then pushed her tongue between my teeth once more.

Eventually we found our way back to the bar, and Anita and I went home. Mary never became my lover—it seems she was nursing a broken heart and felt it was fine to flirt, but no dessert. And Anita didn't do my laundry for a month either, saying that Mary had asked me to dance, not vice versa, so it didn't count. I maintained that it was my looking at her so hard that brought her over in the first place, so Anita should at least do my laundry for two weeks. But she wouldn't.

That was the highlight of the summer of '83. In the car on the way home from the bar, I kept asking myself what in the world ever took me so long. I decided I sure had a lot of kissing and hugging and other things to do to make up for lost time. I'm still working on it.

My Bi Journey

Rachel Kramer Bussel

I'm bisexual, but the process of becoming comfortable
with that label has been a long one. I'll try to start at the beginning. Ever since I was very young, I was interested in feminism. I was always reading my mom's *Ms.* magazines and feminist books. I was very into books as a child and read pretty
much everything I could get my hands on. In the course of my
avid reading, I started reading gay fiction as well as scholarly
books about gay and lesbian rights. This wasn't something
new or strange to me; it was a part of my inquiry into politics
on many levels, and it was in keeping with the open-minded
way I was raised. When I was a teenager, I started reading
Naiad romances by the dozen, but to me they were just fun
books, similar to the straight romances I also consumed. At
that time I had a vast interest in all things gay, but only on a
very abstract level. In other words, I didn't feel some primal
connection to my queer reading; I just enjoyed reading about
something that was interesting—and foreign—to me.

My mom had gay friends and never made a big deal about
whether someone was gay or straight. So I knew about gay
people from the time I was very young—I just didn't think it
applied to me. Sometimes I wished I were gay, because it
seemed "cool" and because being a feisty heterosexual feminist can be hard sometimes. But try as I might, I just wasn't
attracted to women in the guttural, visceral, sends-shivers-
through-my-body way that I was with men, so I left lesbianism for personal study and spent my time naked in bed with
men. I remember working in an office with a guy I ended up

becoming involved with and willing my body to at least be somewhat attracted to my female coworker, but it just didn't happen. I even wrote a letter to gay writer Eric Marcus, who wrote back something along the lines that it was perfectly fine to only be attracted to one gender.

When I went to college at the University of California, Berkeley, affectionately known as Cal, I was bombarded on all sides by radical groups on campus, especially queer groups. At first that world seemed very foreign to me, very bold and in-your-face, and unwelcoming. Those groups seemed to me like the "in crowd" that I wasn't a part of. But in my women's studies classes I was exposed to more real live lesbians than ever before. It was a bit of a revelation because, though I'm sure there were some dykes at my high school, no one I inter-acted with every day was out. The dykes I knew were older, my mom's age, and though I totally loved and trusted them, it wasn't the same as having peers who were queer and proud and loud about it. Those fellow students helped, making me see that if I were queer myself, not only would it be accepted, but it wouldn't really be that big of a deal.

In my women's studies classes we studied theories about why women are oppressed. Much of what we learned I dis-agreed with or thought boring, finding it all much too theo-retical. I wanted things that were sparkling and alive and made me fired up with anger or passion or interest, rather than explanations for women's oppression that still left us mired in that oppression. We spent so much time talking about the myriad problems women face that sometimes I felt we down-played the gains women had made. There seemed little room for celebration of sexuality. I remember one class during my first year in which our professor had us read a piece about how love really oppresses women by making us lose focus on the "more important" goals of our careers. After that reading, which I heartily disagreed with, I found myself thinking more critically, not only about our class readings, but also about life and the world around me. I read voraciously, for class and for myself , but I rarely voiced my opinions.

Sometime around my second year of college (I graduated in only three years, so I would have been a sophomore or junior), I'd started noticing Nicole, who shared many of my women's studies classes. She stood out to me because she was always bold and loud in class, and I knew she was a dyke. She never seemed to share my inability to make controversial statements. She was a bit older than me, 25 to my 19, and seemed to have a world of life experience that I didn't. She had really lived, whereas I felt like the most sheltered person. I liked that she was different from most of my friends, who were living off their parents' money, or wished they were. Nicole had been living on her own for years and knew about a queer life and community I was eager to learn about. We became friends and started hanging out after class, and then after a while we began dating and sleeping together. I know it sounds sudden—it was. We went from meeting at the gym, giggling at the computer lab, and sharing diet Cokes and jelly beans to making out in the street, holding hands, taking showers together, and having sex. We didn't really stop to "define" our relationship, but we were definitely dating. Our relationship only lasted for about a month, but in that time we were very close, and it felt very exciting and heady.

The weird thing about that brief relationship is that I didn't identify as bi at that time. I wanted to, because I wanted to feel a part of Nicole's world, but the word just didn't feel right to me. It wasn't that I was ashamed of dating her or wanted to hide it; I just didn't see how one relationship could change my core identity. Couldn't I be straight mostly and still date her? I definitely liked Nicole, but I didn't feel she was the grand love of my life, that we'd be together forever. Perhaps if I had, my feelings about my own identity would have changed. I didn't think our relationship was an aberration so much as I didn't know where it would lead me, and I didn't want to just proclaim myself a dyke or bisexual because of her. That seemed like a disservice not only to myself but also to those people who were "really" gay or lesbian or bi.

In an interview with *Out* magazine in 1994, Liz Phair called attractions between women "the unspoken taboo of heterosexual women" and was angered at "the lines that have been drawn" between lesbian and bisexual women. Phair was alluding to the fact that there are many straight women who have slept with one, two, or more women of all orientations. At the time I was with Nicole, around the fall of 1995, that's how I saw myself—straight, but attracted to this woman. I believe that it's not the singular girlfriend or act of lesbian sex or any single defining characteristic that "makes" us lesbian or bisexual, but our own internal feelings and beliefs about who we are. I still felt straight, very tough, strong, and independent.

To me, being open-minded about sex and sexual orientation was something that came pretty naturally, and in that way I felt different and apart from many other straight women. Perhaps I was more open-minded and more knowledgeable about lesbianism. Many straight women I knew seemed to partake of a very male-oriented culture with which I didn't identify. I wasn't dating other women or having too many female crushes, but then again I wasn't out having lots of crazy, wild sex with men either. I briefly dated an old boyfriend, then a new one, and Nicole seemed like a singular exception to my rule of dating men. Until, that is, I moved to New York.

After graduating from college at the age of 20, I moved to New York to go to law school. Once I arrived, I was met with a barrage of exciting things I wanted to do much more than studying contracts or torts. Manhattan presented a world of delights, all seemingly at my fingertips, as I lived in Greenwich Village, which I thought of as the epicenter of coolness. I discovered the local indie music scene, which allowed me to go see cool bands every night of the week if I wished, at clubs that were easily within walking distance of my dorm. I also turned 21 and was able to enjoy the benefits of legalized bar hopping. Almost anything I could ask for in terms of socializing, music, art, shopping, and sex were right outside my door.

I was also in the midst of much sexual exploration. For some reason, after years of feeling like I had to let other people pursue me, *I* started to pursue people. I found people who were attracted to me straight off, without my having to go through all sorts of shenanigans to get them to like me as I had in the past. I also bought my first vibrator and starting exploring the world of sex toys. As I slept with more and more men, without a steady relationship, I felt more confident in myself and my body. I don't know if there's a direct correlation between that and the fact that all of a sudden more and more women started to seem attractive to me, but the two did coincide. I found myself noticing women everywhere—at bars, clubs, meetings, bookstores, classes. And not just noticing, but liking them, admiring them, lusting after them. I developed a crush on my best friend, who, after a night of drunken kissing, told me she didn't think we should pursue it. My heart was broken for a little while, but I got over it.

I started to think of myself as bi, even though I still have some issues with that word: I think it implies that there are only two ways to be sexual, with men and with women, when I see infinite ways of expressing our sexuality. I joined mailing lists for bi women and found out about queer happenings around town. I met and made friends with bi and lesbian women, which did wonders for me, because it moved me away from being alone with all my thoughts and desires. I found all kinds of women, in various stages of relationships, who helped teach me that there was no one "right" way to be queer. This helped allay my fears that I wasn't queer or PC enough to "really" sleep with or date women. That might sound silly, but that's how I felt. When I started learning more about butch/femme issues, that further validated me and my quirky femme style.

As I began to feel comfortable with myself, I started to socialize more in the lesbian community and to meet and sleep with more women. Although I wasn't some kind of lesbian Lothario, I did find that I could attract women and that they didn't think I was any different for being bi or not having been out forever. It's also been heartening to see bi women in queer organizations, from magazines to political groups to mailing lists. As a community, we are not as interested in petty labeling as we used to be. In the past few years, I've become more involved in the community by doing political work with a feminist organization, working as an editorial assistant at a national lesbian magazine, and writing stories about and interviewing prominent queer authors. I realized that making and joining communities of queer women was what I had been missing all along. I needed something more inclusive and complex than just the role of the fawning, femme straight girl.

I'm glad I took the time to figure out what was right for me. I know that what I choose to call myself and identify myself as is first and foremost *my* business and *my* choice. I don't need other people to tell me who I am or surmise things about me. If someone wants to know more, they should ask. I'm not out everywhere, but I don't go out of my way to hide being queer. When you're a single, bisexual woman, it's easier to get to know someone first and then come out to them, and I keep my eyes and ears open for places and moments that feel right to let people know—in my own way and at my own pace.

I've grown more comfortable in the lesbian community, especially with lesbian and bi writers. I've found a diversity, honesty, and warmth that I welcome and cherish. Many of the queer girls I hang out with talk about their crushes on men, and it's often not so much in a sexual way as an appreciation of their beauty, the same way we check out other women. I feel most comfortable in the presence of other queer women because I feel there's a commonality that lets me feel free to be myself. And it's not a false commonality, where we have to shed all our differences to bond over what we share, but one where we can discuss, debate, and relish our uniqueness without trashing anyone else's. I've also found almost total acceptance from friends, acquaintances, old lovers, and the members of my family to whom I've come out.

I was at a party the other night, and I realized that just by talking in that breathless, excited, can't-get-the-words-out-fast-enough way I have, that I was coming out to them without having to say "Hi, I'm Rachel, and I'm bi." I was only talking about the girl I thought was cute or running into a guy I liked (and his girlfriend), or about my writing an erotic lesbian story. It would have been awkward to interrupt somebody to say, "By the way, I'm bi." It's just a part of me, not my entire life.

Sometimes I want to be "queer," "gay," "lesbian," "bi," or a "dyke," and I claim my right to be any and all of these. They may signal different things at different times to me, but what I've learned is that I don't need to hide any of my attractions under the rug, catering to this or that faction or person.

My own happiness and comfort is my primary concern, and I'm content with my meandering and ongoing journey of becoming queer.

Angela
Roselle Pineda

For Angela, who I hope someday will find the reason not to cry anymore...

I didn't know what right I had to claim this power to love her, but I did it anyway.

Love always happens when you least expect it, and I was no exception. It hit me one sunny afternoon in mid May of 1996—summer in my tropical country. I had just finished a semester in which I was lacking three units of my teaching load, so I had to teach summer classes in art appreciation to make up those units.

Art appreciation was always a treat for me to teach. For one, it's a subject required of every student, so you get students from all walks of life and various majors; you hear insights from different frameworks—from describing Salvador Dalí using the rules of applied physics to employing geological tools to plot the complexity of Jackson Pollock's abstractions. In my country, being in the field of academic arts almost means starvation; art here is not only a marginalized field but also a burden, as both artist and academic art practitioner have to prove their worth in the society. Since education is a lower priority for our government, being in the field of art means being doubly demonized. And so most of the time we get students who are half-hearted toward the arts; either they're too unfamiliar with them or they're just using the course as a stepping stone toward "more useful" fields like mass communication. I am here, though, to talk about my unforgettable affair with her...unless one would consider her a work of art, which I do.

She was gifted with perfectly polished fair skin and a body so carefully sculpted no one would know that her flat belly had already mothered a beautiful boy, Jerome. I'm on the plump side myself, and I love myself, so I have nothing against large women, but this political correctness about body shapes does not change the fact that I admired her flat belly and her perfectly coned breasts. I was just there to look at her breasts, or rather to glance at them as I tried so hard to look away from her, but I found my gaze glued in her direction.

She stood 5-foot-5. And in the Philippines, this is considered tall for a woman, since we are generally petite. I could never guess the suppleness of her skin, her wide eyes that twitched upward a little in the corners, her small nose and lips that completed a perfectly cute, almost baby-like face. She was crowned by bobcat hair, and her forehead was lined with strays of bangs. She looked like one of those Japanese anime characters—cute, but definitely a woman; petite, but definitely gigantic in person; sweet, but cradling femme fatale qualities within herself.

I didn't notice her right away. She lured me into noticing her. I had just finished my lecture in the class before hers when she came in, looking at me in sheer awe. I took it as both a compliment and a logical reaction toward how I look, because I look different for a professor. I don't wear a bra, and I wear tattoos like a badge of victory, victory for withstanding the pain of getting them done. I enjoy dressing up and looking different each and every day, though I don't wear those tailored suits "fit for a professor."

Once when the dean wanted to talk to me about what I was wearing to class, I said, "Ma'am, you know how important fashion is in this world where everything can be treated as a text, as signs that can be read as representations of power, stature, and gender inequality. Fashion is an art form in itself, and one of the important discussions in my class is to recognize art in our everyday life—yes, including what we wear! We don't expect our students to believe whatever it is we're saying when we don't live it, right? Besides, I'm not only a teacher—I also perform, and this fashion sense is definitely part of the package." I finished my litany about fashion with the sweetest smile I could offer her, and she dismissed me almost immediately after I'd finished talking.

Angela looked surprised when she saw me, and looked even more surprised when she found out that I was to be her professor for the summer. After that first meeting, our class went by like most of my art appreciation classes, with discussions, reports, creative exercises, and field trips. Nothing special happened between her and me. No friction. No chemistry. No special attention was given to her, though once in a while she'd stand up and make a point in class. I always considered her one of my brightest and more articulate students. She was attentive and seemed sure about her opinions about art, while almost all of her classmates seemed to beg me to tell them what to do. Most of all, she was an endearing and beautiful mother.

Angela had a 5-year-old son, and sometimes she would bring him along to class when no one was available to babysit him. For some reason her son loved me, and I was immediately magnetized by him. The whole period was spent talking about Picasso and Rembrandt, and occasionally little Jerome would interrupt me, begging me to carry him on my lap, and I'd oblige. Right there and then, I fell in love with the boy...but his mother was a different story. Only later did I find out that her heart began beating for me the first time Jerome looked up at me with his arms stretched up. Then, she said, she fell in love with me when I smiled back at the child and held him in my arms and gave him a combination kiss-embrace. This, she said, was the moment when she realized she had found everything she wanted in life in me.

Days went by and the laziness of summer caught up with us, so I decided to leave the four walls of the classroom to check out some cultural sites in the region and some dance and music performances at local bars. One night I performed in one of the bars, and she surprised me with her presence. For the first time I felt the dormant tension in my chest. Because of my fear of these kinds of arrangements, I'd never had the courage to cross the boundaries of lure, courtship, and love between a teacher and a student. With a thin line dividing our ages, I do become attracted to some of them, but I'm good at not letting these attractions show since I'm all too aware of the power difference between my students and me, whether I like it or not, and whether I try to break it or not.

I was only two years older than she was, and for some reason I decided that night would be the night to cross that boundary. Maybe it was the transformation of the situation from a classroom setting to an old, shagged bar in the out-skirts of the city. She was there to see me dance, and I was there to receive her. Maybe it was the freedom I felt when I was performing that brought me the courage to let her feel just for a moment the heat I held for her in my chest. Maybe it was the right I'd claimed for myself because that night I was not her teacher, but a performer awed by her audience. I didn't know what right I had to claim that power to love her and let her feel a fraction of that love, but I did it anyway.

We were talking face to face, sitting on a long bench out-side the bar. I faced her directly, while she occupied a more slanted position, so that I could see the expression on her face, but not the entirety of it. We were silent for a long time. Finally she threaded the dangerous ground that separated us.

"So who do you like in our class?" she asked, looking away from me to hide her uneasiness.

"What?!" I answered, astounded and almost unassuming of where she was taking the conversation.

"Well, you're always talking about the handsome boys in class, but you never seem to find any cute girls in class, and somehow I find that queer for someone who says she's queer.

So I want to know, which girls in our class do think are attractive?" She asked this almost casually.

At that point I was choking in my head with my own words. She had observed me accurately. I did make comments about cute guys in class, but I always made it a point not to talk about any girls despite my being out as a lesbian. I was simply afraid to imply any attraction for the girls in my class by giving them compliments. It scared every fiber in my body, and I was very conscious and hard on myself about it. I didn't want to be accused of sexual harassment. Being out as a lesbian did give me a certain sense of empowerment in the political battle of gender, but it also exposed me to certain situations that were very dangerous, like this one. I knew that being an out lesbian already presented an array of dangerous grounds that tempted me to slip, and I wouldn't dare do that—at least, not until she asked me to.

"We're not in the bounds of the classroom, so are you going to tell me?" she continued, with a smirk on her face that told me she knew I was forbiddingly attracted to her.

This woman is playing games with me, I thought, and then said, "No, I'm not going to tell you," in a firm voice.

"So there *is* someone you're attracted to!" she said with a little laugh, as her eyes lit a little bit.

I had incriminated myself. I gave her a small smile, but in my head I was cursing myself for being so vulnerable in front of her. And I had thought I was good at concealing my emotions.

"So, who is she?" Her eyes lit up even more.

"You'll never guess. She isn't who you'd expect her to be...." I tried to save myself from more self-incriminating words by being calm and firm, trying to diffuse her expectations because I knew she was expecting my answer to be her.

If she only knew that I only wanted to touch her face and kiss her so that she could begin to understand how much I wanted her. How much I wanted to make her feel the ache that I felt in my chest every time her eyes lit up or her lips formed words or a crescent smile. How much I wanted to touch her lips with the tips of my fingers, to feel their softness against the coarseness of my skin. I wanted her every time she was present, and every time she was away from me.

I didn't know exactly what had happened between the time that I was trying desperately to conceal my emotions for her and the time I saw her slouching in sadness, ready to drop the bomb on my head. My resistance was obsolete—I found myself telling her how much I wanted to touch her face and kiss her. She was silent for a while, then without looking at me she said, "You know I can't be with you, in that way, I mean. I'm sorry. I'm only attracted to men.... But don't get me wrong—I do like you...." She tried to smile and console me with her last words. But I wasn't hurting. I didn't need consoling, for in my head I had expected that answer from her; I knew her child heart just wanted to push the limits of the game. I knew it really was just a game for her. But it wasn't a game for me.

After that night there was an overwhelming wall of silence between us. We still had three more days before the official end of summer classes, and we spent the last days of the semester in research consultations. Angela didn't show up for any of those consultations, and I was ready for it. I was even getting myself ready for some kind of a scandal after that controversial night. I was preparing myself to tell the university that I stood by my sincerity about what I said to her. But nothing happened.

Then final projects were handed in: a 10-page personal essay, an essay that was the embodiment of whatever they had gained during the semester, about what moved them—a piece of art, an artist, an idea, whatever caught their attention and inspired them. Angela submitted her paper on time, but she didn't write about a piece of art or an artist. Instead she submitted a 12-page handwritten essay about me. She wrote about how my wholeness was an artwork come to life for her, about the way I looked and how she looked at the way I looked when we first met. She told me how I grew to be an artwork in her eyes and described in amazing detail the way I moved, or rather danced, whenever I discussed something. She described the way I seemed to sing whenever I said something.

I tried hard to be objective about the essay and told her something about her having a gift for writing, but all I really wanted to say was how much she had moved me. I didn't tell her that. I was wiser after that night of crazy confessions.

I went away for the remainder of the summer, so I didn't see her after I returned her essay to her. I wanted to have some time to forget her. I was successful for a while in distracting myself from thinking about her, but after two weeks it was time to return and I was faced once again with the fear of seeing her.

Then it happened, as I'd expected: I saw her one afternoon as I was enlisting a group of students in my class. She was lovelier than the last time I'd seen her, when I had planted a kiss on her cheek to say goodbye. She handed me a diskette and told me she wanted me to read what was on it. I went home early to read it, and there it was, the most heartfelt and pained letter I'd ever read. She talked about how much she wanted me to be by her side always, how I was the second mother to her son. She said I was everything her husband wasn't and that she was torn between loving beyond what she was allowed to and not being able to bring herself to act on this love because I was a woman. She confessed that she had manipulated that night of craziness to get me to reveal that I wanted her and apologized for choking, and then told me that given another chance she would be honored to kiss me.

I didn't know what to make of it because after that night at the bar I had become more and more suspicious of Angela and her gestures. I didn't want to make the same mistake of diving in and allowing myself to drown in that kind of moment, showing my vulnerability, especially to someone as unsure about her desires as she was. I didn't answer the letter or exert any effort to see her.

One night she called me at 1 A.M. She was crying in a way

I'd never heard anyone cry before. It was as if she were drowning in her own tears. She was telling me something about her husband between sobs, and though her sentences were cut off by her tears the message was clear: She wanted me to pick her up and take her away from her husband.

What was I to do? A woman who had told me a month before that she couldn't act on her love for me because we were both women called me and asked me to save her—what was I to do? I freaked out and told her I'd call some friends who could help her. Right then I decided never to see her again. I decided I didn't want to have anything to do with her. I abandoned her.

I was hurting when I walked away from her because all I could hear in my heart was a haunting wail that what I really wanted to do was to hold her and keep her safe. But I didn't. I walked away. I stayed away.

Three years later I saw her in the university corridor. Her eyes were red the way they had been three years before. She was with her son, but he didn't recognize me, and she had a pallid and diplomatic expression on her face when she greeted me. I knew she had been cradling anger toward me all these years for abandoning her without even saying goodbye.

I haven't seen her for a year and a half now, but the remorse remains in my heart. I want to beg her forgiveness for abandoning her when she thought I could be her sanctuary. I wonder how she is. Once in a while I write letters to her—I have a box of them in my room. I don't know if she'll ever get a chance to read them. But somehow I think she will some-day, somehow I know our paths will cross again, and by then I'll be ready to face anything she has to offer me—forgiveness, anger, curses, or love—because by that time I'll be ready to take a chance to hear her.

For now I keep one or two letters for her in my pocket, so that when I see her I won't miss out on another chance by walking away without her knowing what or how I felt and feel for her.

I Lost It at the Movies

Jewelle Gomez

My grandmother, Lydia, and my mother, Delores, were both talking to me from their bathroom stalls in the Times Square movie theater. I was washing butter from my hands at the sink and didn't think it at all odd. The people in my family are always talking; conversation is a life force in our existence. My great-grandmother, Grace, would narrate her life story from 7 A.M until we went to bed at night. The only break was when we were reading, or the reverential periods when we sat looking out of our tenement windows, observing the neighborhood, which we naturally talked about later.

So it was not odd that Lydia and Delores talked nonstop from their stalls, oblivious to everyone except us. I hadn't expected it to happen there though. I hadn't really expected "it" to happen at all. To be a lesbian was part of who I was, like being left-handed—even when I'd slept with men. When my great-grandmother asked me in the last days of her life if I would be marrying my college boyfriend I said yes, knowing I would not, knowing I was a lesbian.

It seemed a fact that needed no expression. Even my first encounter with the word *bulldagger* was not charged with emotional conflict. When I was a teen in the 1960s, my grandmother told a story about a particular building in our Boston neighborhood that had gone to seed. She described the building's past through the experience of a party she'd attended there 30 years before. The best part of the evening had been a woman she'd met and danced with. Lydia had been a professional dancer and singer on the black theater circuit; to dance with women was who she was. They'd danced, then the woman walked her home and asked her out. I heard the delicacy my grandmother searched for even in her retelling of how she'd explained to the bulldagger, as she called her, that she liked her fine but she was more interested in men. I was struck by how careful my grandmother had been to make it clear to that woman (and, in effect, to me) that there was no offense taken in her attentions, that she just didn't "go that way," as they used to say. I was so happy at 13 to have a word for what I knew myself to be. The word was mysterious and curious, as if from a new language that used some other alphabet that left nothing to cling to when touching its curves and crevices. But still a word existed, and my grandmother was not flinching in using it. In fact, she'd smiled at the good heart and good looks of the bulldagger who'd liked her.

Once I had the knowledge of a word and a sense of its importance to me, I didn't feel the need to explain, confess, or define my identity as a lesbian. The process of reclaiming my ethnic identity in this country was already all-consuming. Later, of course, in moments of glorious self-righteousness I did make declarations. But they were not usually ones I had to make. Mostly they were a testing of the waters. A preparation for the rest of the world, which, unlike my grandmother, might not have a grounding in what true love is about. My first lover, the woman who'd been in my bed once a week for most of our high school years, finally married. I told her with my poems that I was a lesbian. She was not afraid to ask if what she'd read was about her, about my love for her. So there, amidst her growing children, errant husband, and bowling trophies, I said yes, the poems were about her and my love for her, a love I'd always regret relinquishing to her reflexive obeisance to tradition. She did not flinch either. We still get drunk together when I go home to Boston.

During the 1970s, I focused less on career than on how to

eat and be creative at the same time. Graduate school and a string of nontraditional jobs (stage manager, midtown messenger, etc.) left me so busy I had no time to think about my identity. It was a long time before I made the connection between my desire, my isolation, and the difficulty I had with my writing. I thought of myself as a lesbian between girlfriends—except the between had lasted five years. After some anxiety and frustration, I deliberately set about meeting women. Actually, I knew many women, including my closest friend at the time, another black woman also in the theater. She became uncharacteristically obtuse when I tried to open up and explain my frustration at going to the many parties we attended and being too afraid to approach the women I was attracted to, certain I would be rejected because the women were either straight and horrified or gay and terrified of being exposed. For my friend, theoretical homosexuality was acceptable, even trendy. Any uncomfortable experience was irrelevant to her. She was impatient and unsympathetic. I drifted away from her in pursuit of the women's community—a phrase that was not in my vocabulary yet, but I knew it was something more than just "women." I fell into that community by connecting with other women writers, and that helped me to focus on my writing and on my social life as a lesbian.

Still, none of my experiences demanded that I bare my soul. I remained honest but not explicit. *Expediency, diplomacy, discretion* are all words that come to mind now. At that time, I knew no political framework through which to filter my experience. I was more preoccupied with the Attica riots than with Stonewall. The media helped to focus our attentions within a prescribed spectrum and to obscure the connections between the issues. I worried about who would shelter Angela Davis, but the concept of sexual politics was remote and theoretical.

I'm not certain exactly when and where theory and reality converged.

Being a black woman and a lesbian unexpectedly blended, like that famous scene in Ingmar Bergman's film *Persona*. The different faces came together as one, and my desire became part of my heritage, my skin, my perspective, my politics, and my future. And I felt sure that it had been my past that helped make the future possible. The women in my family had acted as if their lives were meaningful. Their lives were art. To be a lesbian among them was to be an artist. Perhaps the convergence came when I saw the faces of my great-grandmother, grandmother, and mother in those of the community of women I finally connected with. There was the same adventurous glint in their eyes, the same predetermined step, the penchant for breaking into song and for not waiting for anyone to take care of them.

I needed not pretend to be other than who I was with any of these women. But did I need to declare it? During the holidays, when I brought home best friends or lovers, my family always welcomed us warmly, clasping us to their magnificent bosoms. Yet there was always an element of silence in our neighborhood—and, surprisingly enough, in our family—that was disturbing to me. Among the regulars in my father's bar was Maurice. He was eccentric, flamboyant, and still ordinary. He was accorded the same respect by neighborhood children as every other adult. His indiscretions took their place comfortably among the cyclical Saturday-night man-woman scandals of our neighborhood. I regret never having asked my father how he and Maurice had become friends.

Soon I felt the discomforting silence pressing against my life more persistently. During visits home to Boston, it no longer sufficed that Lydia and Delores were loving and kind to the "friend" I brought home. Maybe it was just my getting older. Living in New York City at the age of 30 in 1980, there was little I deliberately kept hidden from anyone. The genteel silence that hovered around me when I entered our home was palpable, but I was unsure whether it was already there when

I arrived or if I carried it home within myself. It cut me off from what I knew was a kind of fulfillment available only from my family. The lifeline from Grace to Lydia to Delores to Jewelle was a strong one. We were bound by so many things, not the least of which was looking so much alike. I was not willing to be orphaned by the silence.

If the idea of cathedral weddings and station wagons held no appeal for me, the concept of an extended family was certainly important. But my efforts were stunted by our inability to talk about the life I was creating for myself, for all of us. It felt all the more foolish because I thought I knew how my family would react. I was confident they would respond with their customary aplomb, just as they had when I'd first had my hair cut as an Afro (which they hated) or when I brought home friends who were vegetarians (which they found curious). While we had disagreed over some issues—for example, my mother and I had fought over Vietnam when I was 19—always when the deal went down we sided with one another. I think somewhere deep inside I believed that neither my grandmother nor my mother would ever censure my choices. Neither had actually raised me; my great-grandmother had done that, and she had been a steely barricade against any encroachment on our personal freedoms, and she'd never disapproved out loud of anything I'd done.

But it was not enough to have an unabashed admiration for these women. It is one thing to have pride in how they'd so graciously survived in spite of the odds against them. It was something else to be standing in a Times Square movie theater faced with the chance to say "it" out loud and risk the loss of their brilliant and benevolent smiles.

My mother had started reading the graffiti written on the wall of the bathroom stall. We hooted at each of her dramatic renderings. Then she said (not breaking her rhythm, since we all know timing is everything), "Here's one I haven't seen before: DYKES UNITE." There was that profound silence again, as if the frames of my life had ground to a halt. We were in a freeze-frame, and options played themselves out in my head in rapid succession: Say nothing? Say something? Say what?

I laughed and said, "Yeah, but have you seen the rubber stamp on my desk at home?"

"No," my mother said with a slight bit of puzzlement. "What does it say?"

"I saw it," my grandmother called out from her stall. "It says, 'Lesbian Money!'"

"What?"

"Lesbian Money," Lydia repeated.

"I just stamp it on my big bills," I said tentatively, and we all screamed with laughter. The other woman at the sinks tried to pretend we didn't exist.

Since then there has been little discussion. There have been some moments of awkwardness, usually in social situations where they feel uncertain. Although we have not explored "it," the shift in our relationship is clear. When I go home, it is with my lover, and she is received as such. I was lucky. My family was as relieved as I to finally know who I was.

Best Friends

Loving Jenny
Alana Corsini

We met during our first year of college. There were four of us—four young women who wanted to be actresses, writers, painters, or dancers. We were at college during the Vietnam era, and while we were politically and socially involved in our times, it was our shared artistic dream that bound us together. Surprisingly, more than 30 years later we have all achieved a version of our early dreams. Jenny and Tilly are actresses who work in television and film in Los Angeles, Mona is a Bay Area painter with regular shows, and I spend a lot of time at my word processor in New York spewing forth novels, poems, plays, screenplays, and articles on the arts.

No self-respecting aspiring artist or intellectual joined sororities in those days, so the four of us rented an old railroad apartment a mile from campus. It had three bedrooms and a glassed-in front porch, which allowed each of us to have a private room. The wallpaper in the dining room featured a gray feather motif against a bland background the color of an internal organ, and the living room couch was supported on one side with empty coffee cans filled with pebbles. It was heaven. I claimed the large bedroom, which could accommodate my double bed, covered with an obligatory Indian-print bedspread. I had a huge slate-top desk; a bookcase filled with poetry and esoteric occult philosophy; and an ancient radiator spraypainted a dull gold. I thought the room struck just the right note between intellectual and erotic.

The late 1960s and early 1970s were touted as an era of great sexual freedom, although this freedom was bounded by the presumption of heterosexuality. Given that one provision, anything else was acceptable. Mona fell in love with the graduate student upstairs and lived with him for years before they married. Tilly went in for serial monogamy. Sex was something she fit in between rehearsals, callbacks, and career planning.

Jenny and I, however, entered the sexual Olympics with great vigor during our college years. It would have required the skill of an air traffic controller to orchestrate the comings and goings of our various lovers. Jenny ran the gamut from a sweet, stuttering fraternity boy to an Italian rock musician she met in Milan to a middle-aged millionaire playboy. I did my part with a bisexual actor, assorted professors (I was an intellectual groupie), a rotund hospital administrator, and an angelic theological student who, in the grip of illicit sex, was losing faith.

Homosexuality, to me, at that time, was associated with ancient Greece, modern French literature, and one openly gay Arab actor I knew at school. As far as it pertained to women, I knew about Gertrude Stein, tough dykes in motorcycle jackets, and Colette's experiences in boarding school. And I considered myself sophisticated.

When we graduated in 1971, our core of four dissolved. Only Jenny and I got degrees; Mona was already off with Ron at another university, and Tilly had dropped out to take up a great career opportunity and got married quickly and directly to her first husband.

I went off to New York to work for a peace/environmental agency by day and an off-Broadway producer by night. It was a lonely year. I had two or three affairs with men I didn't care about and yearned for the closeness I'd had with friends. Jenny was with an improvisational comedy troupe, and we corresponded constantly by letter and tape. Through the months our exchanges became tinged with longing, loss, and a feeling that in our new lives no one knew us as authentically as we knew each other.

After a year in New York, I impulsively decided to move

to Hawaii with two male friends from college and passed through Chicago to say goodbye to my family and whatever friends were still around. I had a strong need to see Jenny and arranged to spend a week with her before leaving for my Pacific adventure.

During the seven-hour drive, I found myself in a state of nervous excitement, belting out torch songs Jenny and I used to sing in college. It was to be a homecoming and an adventure all in one. Jenny. I hadn't seen her in almost a year, and there was nobody I wanted to see more.

Jenny was living in an apartment in an old white frame house with a roommate named Karen, an actress and auto mechanic who carried her own set of VW tools wherever she traveled as a sort of insurance policy against the vicissitudes of theatrical life. When I arrived, Jenny was alone in the apartment, and I was happy for the rare opportunity to have her to myself. She was a Leo and a born entertainer, and tended to gather crowds around her.

At 6 feet, Jenny had a flair for theatrical costume. She concocted outfits from thrift-shop cast-offs, strings of beads, and scarves that suggested a moving caravan. Other times, she'd wear a military or pea coat and stocking cap to create an image of Verushka playing Billy Budd. This day she stood before me unadorned, wearing plain blue slacks and an Oxford-cloth shirt. Her blond hair—which had been rinsed a unique orange-pink shade during her summer modeling in Italy and only now had halfway returned to its natural color—was shorn close to her head. Mannish, I thought, and felt a lurch in my stomach as we hugged and held each other close for a long moment.

We were both physical people—huggers and embracers and touchers—but for the first time there was awkwardness between us. It must have been the long separation, I thought fleetingly. Then we plunged into our stories over countless cups of coffee, and all strangeness vanished. We knew each other. We loved each other. We had years of shared crisis and jubilation and insight and growing up in common. Everything would be fine, I thought.

But it wasn't. The strangeness returned; the strain in the air, the uncomfortable silences. For two days I followed Jenny around in her life. Was it my imagination, or did she purposely keep other people near us most of the time? I went to rehearsals with her. We ate most meals with other actors, and Jenny had the troupe over to the apartment both nights. There was singing and good humor and rarely a private moment.

Finally, very late and long after Karen had gone to bed, Jenny and I would tumble into her bedroom and drop, exhausted, onto her waterbed and fall asleep. Although I had never seen her room before this visit, it felt familiar. She had the wire sculpture from her college room on the wall opposite the bed, and strings of beads and baubles were looped over chairs and racks. I was conscious of keeping my body from touching Jenny as we slept, not wanting to...to what?

I was miserable. Jenny would start to give me a delicious massage on the undulating waterbed, then abruptly jump up to make coffee. Or she'd draw me a hot bubble bath and call me into the bathroom, only to avert her eyes and rush out of the room when I slipped into the water. Something was definitely wrong.

On the third day, Jenny left mid-morning for rehearsal and asked me to meet her at the local pizza parlor for lunch. I lay around most of the morning reading poetry and writing in my journal in an effort to figure out exactly what was going on. I was off to Hawaii on a great adventure, but how come I wasn't thrilled and raring to get going? I decided that it was useless to hang around with Jenny any longer. Maybe now that we were out of college we didn't have that much in common anymore. She was so involved with the theater and her actor friends that there didn't seem to be much room for me. Sharing a past doesn't guarantee a continued closeness, I reasoned. I'd just tell Jenny at lunch that I needed to get a lot of things cleared up in Chicago before I left, and that I couldn't stay the entire week as I had originally planned. She'd understand. We'll always be friends and keep in touch.

Once the decision was made, my mood took a decided turn for the better. I gathered my books together and packed my bag before I started out for the restaurant. I smiled and hummed a tune as I strolled down the street. For the first time, I was aware of the delicate intricacies of the tree branches above me.

When I arrived, Jenny was sitting alone in the corner, resting her elbows on the edge of a table covered with a red-checked cloth. I sat down, brimming with my newly found good humor, and ordered pizza and a Coke. I felt light and at ease and chatted a good deal about nothing in particular. Jenny's face started to brighten. She commented on how I seemed like my old self once again and laughed in her easy, generous way. I was about to tell her that I was leaving that afternoon when I caught the sudden intensity of her gaze. The smile gently faded from Jenny's face. Our eyes locked on each other, and my heart turned over in my chest. I recognized the look in Jenny's luminous brown eyes and the hot feeling coursing through my body. Desire. We both felt it. And we both knew it.

To this day, I don't remember who spoke first, but I remember the simple question: "Do you want to go?" Knives and forks came to rest noiselessly on the edges of plates. Dollar bills drifted onto the table. We walked out of the restaurant, back to the apartment, and directly into Jenny's bedroom in a slow-motion, soft-focus daze. We started to undress singly, then turned to undress each other, shyly at first. We were both comfortable undressing our male lovers, and we were both comfortable with each other. But to undress your best friend as you did a lover was very new. Didn't seduction depend at least in part on unfamiliarity?

We rolled onto the waterbed, and I thrilled to the feel, the smell, the touch of Jenny. Softness, tenderness, and such overwhelming passion. I was half dizzy. We rubbed, we rolled, we laughed, and finally, we shared wondrous tears. Jenny claimed that she now understood why men were so hooked on women's breasts. I suddenly understood that my entire life had changed.

Jenny and I were lovers. All sorts of emotions erupted in me. I, who had been so blasé about my boyfriends, became fiercely jealous of anyone who paid attention to Jenny. When she performed and I saw a man leer appreciatively at her from the audience, I had the urge to turn the table over in his lap and scream, "Back off, you creep! She's coming home with me!" Ah, yes, cool, intellectual Alana transformed into Anna Magnani on a rampage. In my muddled state of wonder, I gave little thought to any future, but as the week wore on Jenny forced me to recognize some hard realities.

Being a lesbian did not appeal to her, Jenny confessed one morning as we were sipping coffee in the kitchen. It had taken her so long to believe she was attractive to men, and she wasn't ready to throw it all away. And she didn't think she could stand being an outcast either. I was stunned. The word *lesbian* had not been formed yet in my own mind. We could both continue to see men, I offered. We both liked men, didn't we? Except we'd have each other as well. Jenny was evasive. Wasn't I about to move to Hawaii? Yes, but that could be changed. After all, everything seemed to have been made new in the past few days. No, Jenny felt that we should each go on with our own lives. Stunned, I had nothing else to say. It was clear that whatever the future was to be, it could not contain the two of us as lovers.

And so, when the week was out, I drove back to Chicago, sold my car, and flew to Hawaii to meet my friends. Slowly I accepted the fact that while Jenny loved me, she was not a lesbian and her life was going to evolve separately from mine.

This affair with Jenny put me in touch with my feelings for women. For years I seesawed between men and women before realizing that while it is easy to get in and out of bed with either sex, what is deepest in me is touched only by another woman.

Sometimes I don't see Jenny for years, but every few months we exchange a long letter or half-hour phone call. She sends me photos of her husband's paintings and of their children—blond and tall as Hitler's youth, she has commented dryly. I send her manuscripts and pictures of me with my lover and our animals. I watch her on television; she reads my work. We still care.

We never mention the week all those years ago when we were lovers. I don't even know if her husband knows about the affair, but I suspect that he'd think it was fine. I wonder, sometimes, if Jenny thinks about our interlude at all, and if so, how she remembers it. I know that, at that time, being a lesbian touched a place of fear in Jenny. I wonder if now that she is secure in herself, she'd remember it as a time of "rounding out" her sexual education, as an expression of love for a friend, or as the satisfaction of a curiosity.

Maybe the next time Jenny and I are both on the same coast at the same time, I'll ask her how she feels about it. And then again, maybe I won't. Her response could not alter in me the bright, bittersweet memory or the quiet joy that continues to come from loving Jenny.

Spring, Finally

Pam McArthur

Spring has come to us finally and I cannot write. The garden has its needs; the field and woods, their pleasures. Brisk, dewy mornings find me on my knees, digging and planting. Clear afternoons call me into the woods, where the buds are bursting on the trees and the air is thick with long-awaited birds. Following a bright flash of orange, I find an oriole building his pouchy nest high in the branches of an oak; pheasants squawk in the undergrowth. Come evening—my usual time for writing—I am bone-weary and too content to wrestle with language, to try to put words to the feelings flowing at the edge of my consciousness. Yet I will try, for spring is the perfect backdrop for this story, with its exuberance of lilac and forsythia, the hidden beauty of pink-edged lady's slipper; this immersion in the world of the senses.

Sweet. This is the first and best word that comes to me when I think of first falling in love, some 30 years ago. Sweet, those months of growing closer, till I breathed in the warm scent of her skin with every breath I took. Sweet, the naïve uncertainty that kept me trembling, not knowing what I wanted, not knowing if she would want it too. And sweet, the touch of feather-shy fingers gradually growing bolder in their wanting.

I want to be clear that the beginning felt like pure love. I want to be clear, because that love was assailed from the very start by the pain of secrecy, then by my parents' unrelenting disapproval, and finally, by my own insecurity and homophobia. It is a miracle to me that the sweetness we knew survived for as long as it did.

We were 16, 17, when it all started. Her name was Peg, and she lived next door. Already we were different from most of the other girls. We spent our time reading horse books and galloping through the woods behind our houses, neighing and kicking up our heels. Weekend nights we spent together, laying down a nest of blankets and sleeping bags on the floor so we could read and talk late into the night. One night she held my hand. It took me hours to fall asleep, and when I woke, her hand was still in mine.

I was very shy about this touching. We never talked about it, and I never knew if it meant as much to her as it did to me. I couldn't bring myself to take the next step—I didn't know what the next step was! For months I bumped into her "accidentally," hoping she didn't mind, thrilled at even this slight touch. Finally, we began to turn toward each other, slowly discovering the delights and passions of our bodies, taking all the time we needed, and making everything up as we went along. I was enthralled; I was ecstatic. I was not good at hiding my desire. Before long, my parents figured out what was happening.

My mother came to my room one night. Without preamble she said, "You must stop being so…intimate…with Peg." My world collapsed under her disapproval. Each day of the next year was filled with tension created by the fear and guilt of knowing my parents hated what I was doing, even while being with Peg felt absolutely right to me. The thrill of sexuality long held back and the desperate defiance I used as a shield added to the pressure.

In the beginning of my senior year in high school, my parents sent me to a psychiatrist. The message was clear: They wanted me fixed. The psychiatrist was noncommittal about my homosexuality—neither passing judgment nor giving support. He did, whoever, recommend that my parents give me a bit more breathing space. This was a relief, although tension still ran high in the house.

I remember vividly the long minutes I spent almost every day on the landing of our staircase—halfway between the safety of my bedroom and the judgment of my parents in the living room. Caught between desire and fear, angry at both Peg and my parents for putting me in this position, I would gather up my courage, take the final steps, and say, "I'm going over to Peg's house." I would be met with stony silence and my mother's pleading eyes. I never knew on which days, pushed beyond her limits, she would say something. Things like:

Where did I go wrong?
We shouldn't have sent you to that all-girls school.
I'll believe it if you're still like this when you turn 30.
I'll give you a dollar for every day you don't see Peg.
Where did I go wrong?

And my father—where was he while this was going on? As I remember it, he left most of the child-rearing to my mother, which was a shame. We could have used more of his quiet philosophy and humor to ease the tension between mother and daughter—twin souls of stubborn self-righteousness. But he is a background figure in my memory of this time, and while he struggled to understand me, my father seemed to side with my mother in thinking that homosexuality was wrong and hoping that I would outgrow this "phase."

My heart was wrenched between my longstanding loyalty to my parents and this newfound love for and loyalty to Peg. I didn't know how to answer my mother's arguments. I had never heard anything to support my belief that my love was both acceptable and beautiful; defending myself was like trying to walk the air between a canyon's walls. I had to build a tightrope of anger and defiance just to survive.

My parents' constant disapproval began to wear me down. I began to doubt I was truly in love. I lay in bed at night, whispering into the darkness: *I love her—I don't love her*. I could not tell which was true. Finally, I decided that I loved Peg for her essence, her spirit—I would've loved her even if she had been a man. I could not reconcile the wonder of loving Peg with the isolation and shame I associated with being gay, so I had to convince myself we were special, not really gay but living some sort of transcendent love.

Even more disturbing was that, having been repeatedly told that what I deeply believed in was wrong, I began to feel dirty. I took that feeling in under my skin. I had a physical sensation of dirt on my hands and believed that I would soil anything I touched. Any friendship, any undertaking, would be ruined if I were a part of it. I still feel the anguish of that time, even now, 30 years later. I still fear rejection every time I come out to someone; I still assume that person will not accept, will not be comfortable with who I am. The young woman who battled with confusing self-hatred is still a part of me, despite all the changes over these 30 years.

And there have been many changes. I went away to college and encountered feminism and gay liberation. For the first time I met people who gave me support, people who encouraged me to be open and proud of being a lesbian. I also became a writer and began writing the stories and poems of my own life, acknowledging and celebrating the world I know. My long relationship with Peg, which sustained me through much of this, finally ended, but I learned that life sometimes gives you a second chance at love. I am now happily entering middle age. I live with my lover, Beth—16 years this winter!—and our 10-year-old son, Aaron, who has changed our lives in ways I can't even begin to describe.

Through all the changes, the process of coming out has skipped and jumped like the thread of a poorly woven fabric. It is a process that will be with me till the day I die. It is not something I am always comfortable doing, but it is the only option my pride allows me. And I find myself thinking about this more and more since I've become a mother. It is imperative to me that Aaron never be ashamed of his family—his wonderful two-mom family—and I can make that possible for him only by example. As we meet the world—other parents at the playground, strangers in the grocery store—I explain our family, and in doing so I feel I am making it easier for us. I am saying that I am proud of our lives. My life.

Rising early this morning, Aaron and I go into the yard as usual. The sun is hot already—spring leaping into summer. We fill the bird-feeder with plump seeds to beckon the cardinals and chickadees, the grosbeak with his sunburst splash of red at the throat. Aaron, not yet 2 years old, delights in calling "Come and get it, birds!" Then he takes my hand and leads me to the flowerbed. Exuberantly, he yells, "The poppies are beautiful! The peonies are great!" as he gently reaches one fingertip out to touch a bursting ball of flower. I am thrilled to see this in him, to see how natural it is for this child to love the earth and all things he meets on it. I vow to encourage him always to respect and love the earth; and most important, I promise to teach him about difference. I hope that, knowing that his family is different, yet wonderful, knowing that his moms are different, yet proud of their lives, he will never be afraid of difference in himself or others; never hide his own unique light, never reject it in others. This is my gift to my son. It is part of my healing of the hurt young woman still inside me. And it is the hope I offer to the future.

The Wedding

Laurie E. Snyder

There she goes. Walking down the aisle. Again.

You'd think I'd be happy. She's my best friend, and I'm sitting up here in yet another balcony playing the music for her wedding. Again.

She looks beautiful. Again. Always. She has the most amazing blue eyes.

He has no idea how lucky he is.

I suddenly have this urge to do an Errol Flynn maneuver. There's a light fixture suspended directly in front of me—one of those cylindrical numbers with four crosses on it that have been standard-issue in every church I've ever been in, regardless of the denomination. It's about seven feet from the edge of the balcony. The top of the light is just about even with the railing.

The last time it was Bach. This time, Mendelssohn. The notes are flying by. I sound fine—even though my mind is on everything but the music. My tone exudes its usual clear warmth. I'm as close as humanly possible to being perfectly in tune with this firewood-quality piano that's accompanying me. The acoustics of the church are wonderful—guaranteed to only make me sound better.

I wonder if I could make it? I'm about 15 feet off the ground.

Reality takes hold. I am not Errol Flynn. And it would not be pretty if I impaled myself on one of the walnut pews down in the sanctuary. It would hurt.

Plus, her parents would not be pleased. They've always liked me, but I suspect that would change if I swung down on a chandelier, scooped up their eldest daughter, and carried her away to live happily ever after.

* * *

The wedding guests will all tell me I played brilliantly. (They did at her first wedding too. Pretty impressive considering how rattled my nerves were that time around. The groom had been a hornist like me. Unlike me, he was a mean cuss who had battered her—something I didn't find out until after she had divorced him.)

This one's "just" a recording engineer. A recording engineer with a job at one of those well-known Hollywood studios you see listed on the back of nearly every record album produced in this country.

No pressure here. You're marrying the woman I love, and you're listening to me with the ears of a critical New York audience. You and your several hundred music friends.

What is she thinking right now? Does she even hear me playing, or is she so nervous she's blocking everything out? What was I thinking when I said yes? Again.

I was thinking about how much I love her. Then and now. So much that, if I can't be the one waiting for her at the end of her walk down that aisle, I can at least play the music that accompanies her. I'm giving her away in the only way I know how.

She has to know how I feel. How could she not?

* * *

We've been friends since college—so close, in fact, that everyone thought we were lovers when we weren't. (She's always been hopelessly heterosexual.)

So close that she's always been able to read my mind. That's why I wanted her to be my accompanist. Without music in front of me, there was always the chance that my nerves would drive the notes from my memory. She always knew when I was about to have a brain spasm on stage. Our respective piano and horn teachers marveled at how well we performed together—at how she could follow me every time I'd forget a few measures. What they didn't know was that she wasn't following me then. She knew, before I did, that I was going to skip ahead.

Does she know how nervous I am now? I'm laboring along here with a piano accompanist who can't follow my lead. My own pianist is up there at the altar getting married. *C'mon, honey. The beat is here. Keep up. KEEP UP. God, it's like dragging a dead horse.*

Our first "encounter with a lesbian" happened right after our first band concert freshman year. One of the seniors we knew invited us back to her dorm room for a drink afterward.

So, in true "Hey! I played well today. Let's celebrate" fashion, Ann and I accepted Liz's gracious offer. And Liz promptly hit on not the lesbian, but on Ann, the lesbian's straight friend. I didn't know I was a lesbian at the time. But my first clue was probably our respective reactions when Liz left to go use the john.

"Is she a…?

"I think so."

"I've never met one before."

"Me neither."

"Umm. Maybe we should go?"

"How come she hit on you and not me?"

That thought lasted about as long as it took us to politely excuse ourselves and head for our own dorm. And then my Evangelical United Brethren upbringing kicked in.

I confess I did not handle it well. Years of being told that "women like that" would burn in hell had taken their toll. I decided it was time to pay a visit to someone on campus who could explain what had just happened. Dave and I had grown up together and had gone through our school district's band program at nearly the same time. I followed him to this particular college because it was a good school, and because my mother liked the idea of my attending college with him. (She thought he'd look after me. On some level, I think she hoped he'd marry me, but we were never anything more than friends. He was more like an older brother.)

"Can I talk to you?"

"Yeah. What's up?"

"I don't quite know how to say this."

"Say what? And where were you after the concert? We looked for you, but you weren't around."

"Um. That's kind of what I wanted to ask you about. We went over to Liz's room for a drink...."

He snickered.

"You knew?"

He shrugged his shoulders in a so-what motion.

"And you didn't tell me?" So much for being the protector my mother had hoped for.

He laughed. "I thought you knew. Everybody knows."

"Well, I didn't know! And neither did Ann!"

"I'm sorry. I just..."

"What?"

No answer.

"What!"

"We all just thought you and Ann..."

"Oh, my God! Nooooooo. No. No. No. We're...I'm...No!"

"Sorry, it's just that you two are always together."

"We're friends! Geez! And define *we*?"

He shrugged.

"Everybody thinks that? Ann's gonna freak when she finds out!" I shuddered. "I can't believe Liz is a..."

"She's not the only one. Most of the people you two have been hanging around with are."

Both of my eyebrows were stretched as far up as they could go.

"Why do you think they call this place Lesbianville College?"

"Why the hell didn't you tell me this *before* I came here? I could've gone anywhere, and I chose *here*!"

Ann took it remarkably in stride when I told her. Clearly better than I had. She actually chided me for being judgmental.

* * *

But she took it a little less in stride when I finally came out to her three years later.

We were driving back from playing a recital at my aunt's church during our senior year. I was feeling good about having just figured "it" out and wanted to share "it" with the world—or at least with that part of the world I thought would be OK with "it."

I couldn't tell her beforehand. Neither of us had ever been to this church so we actually had to pay attention while we were trying to find it. She navigated with a map while I drove.

I couldn't tell her when we were in the church either. It was an evangelical church, and I figured I was tempting fate just by walking through the doors. Mentioning the word "gay" anywhere within the sanctuary would have been too much.

So I told her on the way home.

She nearly drove off the road. And then she recovered enough to say, "No. No, you're not."

I was amused rather than shocked or hurt. This was my best friend. She loved me. I knew this in my heart. I was more devastated later with other friends and family who rent their garments and wailed at the news.

"Uh, yeah. I am."

"No. It's just a phase."

We didn't really say much the rest of the way home.

But true to form, once the newness of the announcement

wore off, it just became a part of who I was for her. Just like my brown hair and green eyes.

We stayed best friends—inseparable all through the rest of undergraduate school and afterward. Still so close that she has always been able to read my mind. We often finish each other's sentences. She even learned to play "Spot the Dyke" during our many trips to concerts and museums and is now actually better at it than I am.

* * *

I've finished the processional. My French horn is resting in my lap.

The love of my life is standing next to her soon-to-be husband.

He's a good guy. Last night at the rehearsal dinner, he even pulled me off to one side to ask my advice. Seems he's had trouble getting comfortable with her father and wanted to know how I'd managed it.

Yes, he knows I'm a lesbian—and that I'm her best friend. She told him somewhere along the way, and he was OK with it. Still is.

Her father, on the other hand, has no idea, which is probably why he likes me. Well, I'm not even so sure about that. After her divorce from the ex who was abusive toward her, her dad was so happy to have me around to take her mind off things that he made me feel like part of the family for the first time in all the years I'd known him. I still remember how he walked me out to my car as my visit was ending. He checked under the hood to make sure everything was in working order and then gave me the biggest, longest bear hug I'd ever experienced. Ann was amazed. She told me later her father had never hugged anyone like that. Much as I wanted to read something into that embrace, though, I knew it wasn't a "take my daughter, please" moment.

So, I wasn't quite sure what to tell her soon-to-be husband at first. I hedged. "I think it just takes time. I've known them forever. Her dad didn't really start to warm up to me until after college."

Soon-to-be didn't want to wait.

"You know how badly her first husband hurt her, don't you? I mean, she did tell you?"

He nodded.

"Well, her parents are reluctant—understandably—to see that happen again."

"But I love her," he said. "I'd never..."

"I know you do, but he said the same thing too. And he nearly destroyed her. They're just...wary."

He nodded—more thoughtfully this time.

"I'd say just give it time. They'll grow to trust you. There is one thing you should know, though."

"What?"

"I'm wary too," I said. "I won't go through that again with her. I always felt badly for not knowing how horribly her first marriage was going—for not doing more to help her through it. She didn't tell me, but I still should have sensed something. She's my best friend. I won't make that same mistake again. If you ever hurt her, it's not her father you'll have to worry about."

He raised an eyebrow.

"I don't know you all that well," I continued, "but I do know her, and I know she loves you. And because she does, there must be something pretty special about you. She's a rare breed. She's bright, she's talented, but most of all, she has a good heart. She is one of the most caring, genuinely decent people I know. She deserves someone who will appreciate all of those qualities and who will always be there for her. Promise me you'll take care of her."

He nodded.

* * *

The minister just reached the audience participation part. I could stand up right now and say something.

Tell me what to do. Can't you hear my thoughts? Do you know I love you more than anything? You've always known when I'm sad or scared. Even when we've been hundreds of miles apart, you've called when you sensed something was wrong—and you were right! Can't you feel this pain in my chest right now?

Thank God for short Protestant ceremonies. Her last one was a full-length, marathon Catholic wedding. I nearly died.

It's an effort to fight back the tears. I have such a lump in my throat, and now I have to play the recessional so they can walk out together, hand in hand!

I smile lamely at the pianist. Fortunately, she chalks up my red nose and moist eyes to the classic wedding tears of joy.

We finish playing after the bride, groom, and the horde of guests pass under the balcony. I putter around, delaying the inevitable first sighting of the happy couple as long as possible. I finally make my way down the staircase, being stopped by every other guest to shake hands and nod awkwardly or blush at their comments about how well I'd played.

She sees me across the room before I see her. The crush of people makes it impossible for us to do anything more than smile at each other.

She's beaming.

So is he. Actually, if truth be told, I like him. If I had to hand her off to anyone, he's probably the best choice. He loves her and cares for her—probably better than I ever could.

Maybe she already had read my mind? Maybe that's why, when she asked, I played. Again.

One Sunday

Candyce Rusk

I remember the warm Sunday afternoon distinctly. It was in the mid 1960s—I don't clearly remember the year—but oh, that hot afternoon! I lived in a small Midwestern town along the shores of Lake Michigan. Pam, the 15-year-old blond femme fatale of my neighborhood, was with me in my parents' guest room. I was about 13 and all fire and tomboy, hating hair curlers and playing kick the can with the boys.

Pam had big blue eyes, a full toothy smile, and wore her newly developed figure with a definite pride. Kick the can didn't interest her, even though she was a fast runner. I was, frankly, on the edge of a strong attraction to her, and very shy.

Shades and curtains drawn, we lay on the divan amidst popcorn and newspapers, eagerly waiting for the world premiere of *The Three Stooges Go to the Moon*. As the opening credits rolled, Pammy turned to me, fluttering her eyes. She placed her newly polished pink fingernails on my thigh. I feigned indifference, though excited by this unusual move. My mind flipped to Annette Funicello, the cutest and best-developed Mouseketeer. I had a strange feeling about Annette—a feeling I know now as attraction and, well, adolescent lust. But here was Pam, her fingers running down my leg, slowly.

She turned. "If you had to be a Stooge, which one would you be?" Her voice chimed in my head.

"Oh, Moe," I answered quickly. "He doesn't get hit as much and he's the big shot."

"Really, now, Moe—that hair," she replied. "At least

yours is blond." Her arm smoothly encircled my shoulder. Moving slow as molasses, her fingers moved up my neck.

As the Stooges raced around on the screen, my young heart thudded loudly in my chest. I closed my eyes and hoped my brothers and sister wouldn't barge in.

"Where's the newspaper?" Pam asked, suddenly moving away. She grabbed the paper off the floor, her madras pants pulling tight and revealing her smooth upper backside. I thought briefly of temptation and sin, being a Catholic, and then pushed it from my mind.

"See this?" Pam's long finger was fixed on a movie ad from a James Bond film. A seminude model was reclining seductively on a couch, her head close to the floor, her breasts on the edge, pointing majestically upward.

"Yes, I see it," I said gruffly. "What about it?"

"She's beautiful, don't you think?" questioned Pam.

"Sure," I answered, struggling to remain cool. What was she getting at, anyway? According to the nuns at school, anybody who saw a James Bond film was a "pagan." Pam was a Lutheran and obviously going to hell, unless I could convert her to the Catholic Church. Given the way things were progressing, that seemed highly unlikely.

"Let's play James Bond." She faced me fully, her chest heaving with excitement. "You...you be James Bond, and I'll be her—the girlfriend." She reached gently for my glasses and slid them under the divan. The world went soft around the edges. Squinting, I watched as Pam's arms crossed in front of her. She pulled off her sweater. Such a rib cage! And her bra! All lace. I'd only seen bras like that on the mannequins at Penney's Department Store downtown. Certainly I didn't own one. I was glad she was playing the girlfriend—she was so well equipped for the part.

"Now..." She got up and opened a closet door. "A gown, or a robe." Pam pulled out a gaudy black negligee someone had given my mother as a joke. She put it on. The top half of

Pam was all woman. The bottom had pants that stuck out merrier than twin plaid Christmas trees. Still, I was duly impressed.

"All right." She moved, standing directly in front of me. "You go into the closet and act like you just came back from a spy mission." Getting up, I gave her a wide-eyed look, fully aware that this was far more serious than our usual pretend games.

Once inside, I heard the muffles from the Three Stooges soundtrack. Pam was positioning herself with great pains on the couch, judging from the sound of things. I felt silly and flushed in the dark closet. A strong pulsing of blood wound its way through my body. Would Pam want me to kiss her? I didn't have any practice, except when I kissed my own wrist.

Finally she called me out. "All right, James...Mr. Bond... come in, please." I filled my chest with air, simulating a burly strength. I wouldn't find out till years later that Bond was suave and slim.

I strode out of the closet, surprised and deeply delighted at Pam's invitation. Her gown was open, her breasts pointing majestically upward. I froze, unsure.

"On top of me," Pam breathed, air stuck in her throat. So I lay on top of her...just like that. Pam's upside-down face was turning red. "Come *on*, dummy." I responded to that request. I lay down on her, feeling her warm curves and bones. My face was in line with her breasts. Pam sighed. I thought I was squishing her.

"Now kiss them." Plural. That meant two. That meant her breasts. Oh, my God. I bent down, my lips nuzzling along the edges of her lace bra. I was aware of their soft sponginess. "Now pull it down," Pam urged. I tugged gently and her breast jiggled, waiting to be set free. Sympathetically, Pam pulled her bra up. I stared at her nipples, such a light soft pink. I felt them looking at me. "Kiss them." I kissed. So soft. So warm. So Pam. "Now circle them with your finger."

Slowly I outlined her breasts, shuddering, truly amazed at the sensuality of this game. My own breasts were tingling, as was the lower half of my body. I wanted her hand there, touching me. Pam moaned and we melted into each other.

From out of nowhere, my little brother shouted, "Hey, open up, you guys!" I guiltily slid off of Pam, sideways. She fell to the floor, her bare half disappearing from me. "I wanna watch the movie, you TV hogs!" my sibling screamed from the far side of the world. Pam, flushed and insulted, hissed at me, "James Bond doesn't have any brothers!" She quickly adjusted her bra, and removed herself from my mother's nightgown. As she grabbed for her sweater, my heart sank. I realized I had crossed some border and was forever changed. I'd had a confusing but sweet glimpse at sensuality, the gentle give-and-take of desire.

Later the sultry day became evening and the sun turned a deep red. Pam and I rode our bikes to the Dairy Queen on Main Street. I insisted on buying her a cherry-coated vanilla cone, perhaps because it reminded me of her soft, soft breasts.

I didn't know that Pam would turn quickly to boys after our encounter, excitedly relating to me stories of her sexual progressions. I stayed spinning in a state of desire for her, ready and waiting for another cue that never came.

Years later, when both of us were in college, I visited Pam at her apartment for the weekend. As we lay together on a double mattress on the floor, she turned to me. "Ever make it with another girl?" she asked offhandedly. It dawned on me that the rite of passion we had shared was buried somewhere in her subconscious. "I've fooled around a bit," I sighed, "but I guess it wasn't serious." We turned from each other then, our sharing forever sealed. Listening to a Buffalo Springfield album, my mind wandered back to the old neighborhood. Hard rocket baseballs, kick the can, the Three Stooges, the Beatles. How may people are able to associate an erotic memory with the Three Stooges? I can—that warm Sunday afternoon with Pam.

You Must Not Be Doing It Right

Liz O'Lexa

Coming out is not a singular, one-time event. Whenever we step from being another face in the crowd toward being an individual who has a name and a personality, we're again faced with the decision of coming out. And again and again, as long as we continue to have the defiance to exist. We don't all dye a purple streak down the middle of our hair, quit our job, start a *womyn*-owned business, and secede from the patriarchy by embracing lesbian separatism, although I know one dyke who did.

The beginning of my journey was coming out to myself. It happened in 1975, when I was 14 and my knee touched the knee of the most beautiful woman in my Minneapolis high school, Julia, and I felt an undeniable surge of sexual excitement. All of my life experiences seemed to come together at once, and I knew I'd discovered the core of myself. I finally saw all that I'd been feeling in a new, sexual light, and I found the word for myself: *lesbian.*

I could go on endlessly about Julia, how much this first love meant to me, how I wanted to spend the rest of my life with her, how she was intelligent, athletic, absolutely beautiful, and completely unattainable. My first love never became anything more than a sweet fantasy that filled my mind throughout high school. Once, I kissed her on the cheek—a terribly brave gesture, because social kissing, even at Christmas, was something that took place in another world.

Years later, I wondered why I was so frightened of telling her how I felt. I thought for a while that it was racism, since she was black and I white and our worlds outside the classroom were strictly segregated. I'm honest enough to admit that might have been part of the reason, but most of it was that I was afraid. I was lonely and refused to risk having the one and only fantasy that kept me company pulled out from under me.

Just before we started college, I did come out to her. But I didn't have the guts to tell her then that I loved *her*, Julia, the woman who was still to me the most beautiful, gentle, desirable woman on earth, and who'd also become deeply entrenched in the "cool" crowd, smoking weed and sleeping with me. Seven years after our knees first touched, I ran into her on a bus, and at the end of a long ride I told her that she was my first love. We bravely hugged each other during the middle of rush hour in a rather rough section of downtown.

The very first time I actually told anyone—the first time I ever said *lesbian* out loud—was completely unplanned. I was 17, in my senior year, and I'd landed an incredible job as one of the editors of a student-operated tabloid newspaper. We were the crème de la crème of up-and-coming high school journalists pulled predominantly from the best schools.

We—six other student editors, our very hip adult editor in chief, and I—were in the midst of a pre-brainstorm session lunch. I was seated across the table from a man who was to become a longtime friend (and would later come out himself) retelling a stunt pulled at school: Someone had pasted a KISS ME, I'M GAY sign on someone else's back. Our very liberal editor in chief said rather quietly but firmly, "We don't think those kind of jokes are funny because one of our staff is gay."

I just about crawled under the table. *How did she know about me?* Then, as my internal panic subsided, I realized: *There must be someone else who's gay! I'm not the only one!*

I looked cautiously at each person at the table and placed my bet on a then shorthaired, rather butch-looking woman, our photography editor. Later, I found out that I was wrong;

Katie was from an avant-garde family and was just a couple of years ahead of the androgynous look. The point is, I *had* to know who it was, and since I couldn't be sure by guessing the only way I thought I could find out was by revealing myself.

In the car on the way back to the office, I told our editor in chief that I was a lesbian. She nearly drove the car onto the curb and gave me the most unequivocally positive response I've ever received—particularly when she found out that it was the first time I'd told anyone.

When we reached the office, she introduced me to David, the other gay person on the staff. He later introduced me to gay theater in Minneapolis and long soul-searching talks unlike any I had had before. The editor assured me that everyone on staff was tolerant, if not supportive, and I decided to make an announcement, to get my coming out off on the right track. Impulsively, I stood on a chair to announce my lesbianism, an honesty equaled only by marching in the New York pride day parade. After our meeting was over, as we were leaving the building with the sun setting dramatically, David bid me farewell by proclaiming, "Welcome out!" It was an extremely positive, unusual, and good start.

Like a snowball rolling down a mountain, I kept coming out to the important people in my life. During one of our soul-searching talks on the telephone, David convinced me that I should tell my parents. He planned on telling his, and he knew his mother, who loved him very much, would take it well. Besides, being closeted to your own parents smacks of a dishonesty that shouldn't exist in a good parent-child relationship.

In another bravado gesture, I asked David to hold the phone. I walked into the living room, where my parents were watching *Charlie's Angels*, turned down the sound on the TV, and said, "Mom, Dad, I have to tell you something. I'm a lesbian."

My father replied, "Bullshit. Turn the sound back up."

I told them that I knew it was difficult for them to accept and asked them to think about it for a while, and that I'd talk about it later. Then I hightailed it back to the phone and the safety of my room. Talking to David then gave me the courage to go back out and face my parents 20 minutes later.

Mom, Dad, and I talked for a long time, and we cried a little too. But they eventually reaffirmed what I'd always known: that they love me very deeply and will always be my staunchest supporters. After much pleading and cajoling, three years later they marched in my first gay pride parade with me, carrying a sign that said WE LOVE OUR LESBIAN DAUGHTER. Appropriately, that year, 1981, the theme of the parade was "Love in Action." Later, Mom said she had no regrets about it—except that it took three days for her girdle to dry out.

Since I had all this unbelievable support, one would expect me to be unrealistically happy, but I wasn't. I was out to my coworkers, my parents, and myself but I had yet to actually have a relationship with another woman. I was still incredibly lonely and wanted to become a part of the city's lesbian community. At first it didn't seem necessary to come out into the lesbian community, but in reality it was. I had to assert myself and find a place to fit in.

There were no lesbian bars in Minneapolis, and though there was one women's bar in St. Paul it was out of the question, since it was more than two hours away by bus. There was, however, an alcohol-free space called the Women's Coffeehouse. After discovering it, it took me about a year to find the nerve to go there. In the meantime, I found the Amazon Bookstore, my refuge from the overwhelmingly straight world. It supplied me with tons of reading material and lesbian-positive images, but it was hardly a social nucleus for me.

My experience in "the lesbian community" got progressively more negative, because everyone, myself included, was uncomfortable with my young age. When I did make it to the Women's Coffeehouse, I was shunned because I was a stranger. Everyone was already quite well organized into cliques. I searched on until I discovered a building called the Lesbian Resource Center, and I joined the coming-out group. I thought it wasn't appropriate, since I was already out, but it was a way to meet other lesbians. Unfortunately, the friendships didn't last too long. As a first-year college student, I had little in common with women concerned about their careers, house-buying, and their long-term relationships with lovers.

I tried fitting into the "politically correct" community. I joined the brand-new *Lesbian Inciter* newspaper collective. At the meetings, I was confronted with the process of consensus, the ideals of separatism, more ageism, and the politics of class.

But I was still very much on the outside, and *lonely*. After meetings, the women broke up into cliques and ignored me. At that point, it would have been more meaningful if someone had asked me if I'd had a nice day than about my experience in the patriarchal university. But no one ever asked me if I'd had a nice day *or* how my classes were.

Then I joined a small single-lesbians' group, which was composed of the few *Lesbian Inciter* women who weren't in monogamous couples, none of them under 40. Most of them were into discussing their unfulfilling, short-lived relationships. And there I was, still looking for my first one! I made the decision then to leave that group the night one woman said she didn't masturbate because it just wasn't as good, wasn't as "fulfilling" as having a partner. Speaking as someone who'd done nothing but masturbate, during the break I put my arm around her and whispered, "Diane, about masturbation: You must not be doing it right."

Years later, I heard about something called "internalized homophobia," which is learning to hate yourself and distrust those around you because society hates you. Phobias are fears. Straight people who fear queers are dangerous enough, but when we begin to fear each other and consequently ourselves, we create a divided community open to only a select few. Homophobia makes *them* want to lock us away from *them*, but it also makes *us* want to lock *us* away from ourselves and each other.

I consider myself lucky. I am supported and loved by the many important people in my life, friends, and family, and in retrospect I can almost understand why I wasn't welcomed with open arms into a community where I felt I belonged. Ultimately, I did have my first sexual experience, and I've even had a couple of monogamous relationships. I moved to Baltimore, where I'm currently living, and found a "new" lesbian community completely different from that of Minneapolis. I've heard that the Minneapolis community is much changed now and includes dykes even younger than I was.

Ironically, Minneapolis does seem friendlier now that I'm living in Baltimore. It could be because the lesbian community has changed, or because as I age I become more comfortable with myself. Or it could have something to do with my last visit, when I seduced one of the most beautiful women in the Twin Cities area. Most likely, it's because I'm learning that there is not a "right" or "wrong" to coming out. My lesbianism is an integral part of my individuality, and each time I assert myself I come out, sooner or later. My coming-out story is my life story, which is harder to end than it was to begin. Since coming out is a lifelong process, there's always the possibility of a new beginning.

Married Life and Later

Crone Story
Emma Joy Crone

For me, coming out has been a continuous, growing, empowering experience—not something I can intellectualize, but a political, philosophical, and emotional way of life.

Nineteen sixty-eight found me in San Francisco, long before it became the city of freedom for homosexuals that it is today. I was newly divorced after 12 years of marriage, newly immigrated, looking for a new husband, and not at all interested in the feminist movement that was in full swing around me. I was resisting the suggestions by my friend Louise that I "go to a women's meeting." I did not want to be one of those women wearing blue jeans; I was 40 years old and thought I was pretty set in the way of life that I had known all those years. However, I had always been a political being, and the fact that the invasion of Cambodia was happening and much was developing around this issue in the U.S. prompted me to go with others from my place of work to a workshop in Berkeley entitled Women and Work. At this workshop, a feminist (unrecognizable as such to me because of my preconceptions) talked of what was happening on campus with women's issues. Doors flew open in my head, and on returning to my place of work, I announced to my friend Louise that I was interested in going to a consciousness-raising group. One visit and I knew that I had always been a feminist—little did I realize that this was to be my first step to coming out.

My life up to this time had been spent in an industrial city in England. I had never heard the word *lesbian*, but when I was a young woman someone had pointed out a pub where "those women" went. When I asked what this meant, my friend said,

"If you go in there and sit down, they will come and talk to you and touch you on the leg"—this was my basic introduction to lesbianism. I didn't hear the word until I became involved in women's issues. Never before had I been exposed to any of the depressing, sad, inhibitory, homophobic stories I have heard since then. Sex when I was growing up meant babies, nothing more. As with many people of my generation, the joys of sensuality or sexuality with either sex were never made known to me—let alone the fact that I could enjoy my life as a woman loving women in a way totally unimagined to me.

On looking back now, it feels to me that my immigration to the U.S. at the age of 40 was the real beginning of my life. My first three months were spent in the city of New York. What an experience! My life as a heterosexual in a repressive culture of working-class attitudes toward life and marriage had left me totally unprepared for the attitudes and openness I found working as a floating secretary in one of the largest cancer research establishments. The first office I worked in was with a gay man and a woman of color who thought I was a hoot because of my English expressions, and learning the American language proved to be a constant challenge of new expressions and misuse of words, such as *rubber* for *eraser*. The other major difference, which to me at that time was very important, was the attitude toward divorce. In England, I had literally been shunned as a divorced woman in places I'd worked, and I felt I had failed in this aspect, then important to me, of my life as a woman. However, in the U.S., the reaction was "Is it your third or your fourth divorce?" I was stunned, and while nowadays I have a very different outlook on this attitude toward marriage, at the time it was a very freeing experience. In my background, one where one kept the marriage vows and did not look at another man (let alone a woman), I can only now see that my marriage was a very dull and forbidding experience in my life.

I stayed in New York for three months; on hearing of the

awful winters they experienced there, I decided to take a plane to sunny California. Incidentally, I should say at this point that during the whole of this adventure, I knew no one in the United States. I had taken off from England in a very sad, depressed state, convinced that my life was over and that I would just find another husband and, hey, presto, all would be well.

San Francisco at first was not too exciting: Jobs were hard to find, and agencies were charging large fees to put one in touch with an employer. I lived in a Catholic hostel for women, this being the cheapest place that provided huge breakfasts, part of which I would take to work with me for lunch! I finally found work in a large teaching hospital, and it was there that I met Louise. We worked in the same department, had coffee breaks and lunch together, and spent many weekends at either her home or mine. Everyone was talking about us, waiting for "it" to happen.

Once I had discovered myself as a feminist, I then became involved in many sharing womanly projects that were happening around me. It was a time of great excitement and opening up for me, as for many other women at this time: skills taught by women, art, meetings, self-defense classes, and empowerment around the issue of rape. Women were opening their homes to do projects in. I met many wonderful women, but my awareness that I was mixing with lesbians did not come till much later. Louise and I used to go to gay bars, as well as hang around with lots of women. In those days there was no Amelia's or Mama Bear's or coffeehouses for women. We just sat watching at the women's dances we went to, never dancing together, until one night when we finally decided to try it out. I must mention at this time that, though feminist and involved with all these woman-oriented happenings, we were still relating to, and sleeping with, men. I cannot believe nowadays that I could have been so naïve as to not realize that many of the women with whom we related were lesbians. No one ever tried to initiate us into lesbianism—contrary to societal belief about homosexuality.

One day Louise and I were out driving, and right out of the blue I said to her, "Have you ever wondered what it would be like to make love with a woman?" She gripped the steering wheel hard.

"I don't know" was all she answered, with no more discussion.

She was extremely quiet for the rest of the day, and I felt I had made a faux pas and did not pursue the subject. I had no idea where my question was coming from. We'd neither of us during our growing-up time had the freedom to express our needs, sexual or otherwise. So discussions around sexuality were still taboo, and as I've said before, relating in a sexual way to women was something neither of us had heard of. Louise, who was also 40, had been brought up Roman Catholic, and my upbringing, though not religious, had been completely devoid of any knowledge about sexuality.

One weekend when I was home in bed on a Saturday night, there was a knock on the door. Louise and our gay male friend had just been to Kelly's Bar (this was in San Francisco— 45 miles away—I was living in Sonoma County) and had decided to drop in and see me. We talked awhile (it was midnight), and then a discussion as to where to sleep ensued. The gay man decided on a piece of foam on the floor, and Louise jumped into bed with me. Neither of us was prepared for what happened, for that night I caressed a woman for the first time in my life. We didn't make love in the sense of genital sex, but we realized we were women loving each other. The next morning I was overwhelmed with delight, for not only could I be close with women as a feminist, I could actually be lovers with women. I wanted to shout from the housetops; it was the most wonderful, amazing thing that had ever happened to me.

I was so elated with this new aspect of my life that on going to work the following Monday I rushed into a department where I knew a young lesbian technician and burst out with my news. Then came my first introduction to homophobia.

"Hush," she said. "You mustn't tell everyone, people don't like us." Back then I could not understand why; since then, I have learned much about society's attitudes. To this day, I am not ashamed. I have no sense that there is anything wrong in my being a lesbian; it feels the most natural way of life to me. If people don't like who I am, they don't have to relate to me. There are many wonderful lesbians in the world, so I don't feel the loneliness that many lesbians in the past have had the misfortune to experience.

I have met many lesbians while traveling in Europe and living on women's land in the United States, Denmark, England, and Canada, where I now live.

One of my greatest coming-out experiences was in Oregon, where in 1977 I went to a Gathering of Old Women (I was 49 at the time) happening in Wolf Creek. I went to find my peers, and there discovered myself as a writer, a spiritual woman, and most exciting of all, a countrywoman. I had never thought I could once again find a new lifestyle, and one that was more conducive to my way of living and happiness than I had yet experienced. I learned many new skills (once again from women); I learned that I did not have to have bulging muscles to chop wood, and that I had peer-counseling skills. Other women showed me how I hid my fears, and how to be a real person in my relationships with women. I felt safe to explore myself as a human being, letting go once again of many misconceptions about myself. Many workshops and many months later, I returned to Canada filled with a sense of selfhood. In Oregon, I formed nonsexual relationships with many new women who have since become my "family"—but I call them my tribe. These lesbians now live in many parts of the world, and I have a tribal family with whom I keep in constant contact. It sure beats the life experience I had before the age of 40.

Country living has become for me the life I want to live for as long as I am on this planet. I see this as coming from my childhood, for when I was growing up in a smoggy, polluted

EMMA JOY CRONE

city, I used to escape to the countryside, youth hosteling every weekend. The youths I was with, on looking back, were always women. I see that my life has constantly been woman-oriented, and though I never thought about it until writing this, I, like many others, went through "crushes" on two of my school-teachers—one the gym mistress (as they were then known) and the other my English teacher, who, I remember, had beautiful red hair and was called Miss Frost (*sigh*). Country life has meant that I have time to develop my skills without city distractions. I am busier than I have ever been. While always being open to challenge and learning more about myself and the world around me, I feel this is the reason that lesbianism is not hard for me. I love life, and at 60 years old I now feel I am entering new phases, new beginnings. I recently had my first article published, I am working on watercolors, and I am taking drawing lessons. For the past four years, I have been putting out a newsletter aimed at increasing the visibility of older lesbians, hoping that this would encourage others to share their life experiences, dreams, and visions of alternatives for their future as elders to those presented by current society.

I live on one of the Gulf Islands of British Columbia, and while this can be isolating, I fill my time adequately. I have now been celibate for three years, by choice. This is not because I no longer want to love and be with women, but because I am going through a healing process—for with awareness comes the understanding of what I have been doing with most of my life, some of which has of course been quite hard to cope with. In particular, I think of menopause, that other time when I discovered my fears around aging. I found myself once again alone in that many of the women around me were younger or had had hysterectomies, and the whole of literature I discovered was written by male doctors who considered this episode in a woman's life an affliction best ignored or doused with tranquilizers. Now there are many books written by and for women on this very different change in our lives. At that time, I took myself off to a cabin in the country, where I lived alone, grew a garden, and had my hot flashes and pseudoarthritic pains and depressions. Gradually, over a period of years, I adjusted (once again) to yet another process of change in my life.

Self-discovery and personal growth work have been my constant companions, with lots of therapy with wonderful spiritual feminist lesbian workers thrown in. I use the word *workers* rather than *counselors* because it is all work! This continues where I live now, where I am involved with another women's group—adult children of dysfunctional families (but that is another story).

I am now meeting, through my newsletter and output to various magazines and my writing, some older lesbians. Many have grown up with the knowledge of their lesbianism, and some have worked as professionals or in jobs that have not enabled them to be "out" in the world; this can make for a lot of fear about coming out. There are others who, while recognizing their love for women, are trapped in the so-called security of marriage. However, to all these women who may be afraid of the label of *lesbianism* and the connotations that society has placed on this word, I would like to say that there is joy and strength to be gained in the knowledge of oneself. As we age, why not be as we are meant to be, instead of a reflection of what others desire?

One woman I met through S.A.G.E. (Senior Action in a Gay Environment coming out of New York) lived alone and was referred to this organization by a social worker after having been in the closet all her life and with a partner. She said, "If I can't come out at the age of 92, when can I?"

The more of us that reveal ourselves, the more society will have to accept our presence. We are a living force to be reckoned with.

SO CRONES, COME OUT, COME OUT, WHEREVER YOU ARE!

To Me, With Love

Jenny Gafny-Watts

"The aim of life is self-development. To realize one's nature perfectly—that is what each of us is here for. People are afraid of themselves, nowadays. They have forgotten the highest of all duties, the duty that one owes to one's self."

—Oscar Wilde, *The Picture of Dorian Gray*

I am a lesbian, a woman who loves women—one woman in particular—and a woman for whom the idea of ever again *giving* herself to a man (not that I ever truly gave myself in the first place) is too far-fetched to even warrant contemplation. How long have I been a lesbian? All my life. When did I come to terms with my sexual identity? When I could no longer ignore the pain and loneliness associated with masquerading as a bona fide member of the straight world. In other words, some time approximately two years ago when, at the age of 40, I finally realized that being true to myself—whatever the cost—was the most precious gift I could ever bestow upon those I love, myself included.

But what was it, exactly, that brought me to face reality head on, to divorce my husband of 15 years, to fight for custody of my three children and come out as a lesbian? The answer is simple: I finally experienced the one thing for which I had longed my entire adult life, the one thing for which my soul and body ached, the one thing I had almost given up hope of ever experiencing: pure, unconditional, and all-embracing love. And the source of that love? Myself. I finally learned to love myself, and to respect myself and my rights as an individual, and to do what was best for *me,* albeit with the help of the most amazing woman alive, my partner, Nili.

I have to admit that my coming out was a long process. As a teenager I often had crushes on women but attributed them to nothing more than my having only a casual—but outwardly enthusiastic—interest in men and a wild imagination. In reality, the more I was with men, the more I realized something was *missing.* Yet for reasons I've never really understood or cared to admit, I kept trying to convince myself that being with a man while craving the touch, smell, feel, and companionship of a woman (and even in a couple of instances actually *experimenting* with women) was *normal* and in no way suggested I was gay. Looking back, I should have gone with my instincts from the very beginning but, as fate would have it, there was an additional complication to consider. I was told when I was still quite young that I couldn't bear children; in spite of that earth-shattering news, I remained determined to one day become a mother. Perhaps that, more than anything else, motivated me to ignore my "unnatural" natural desires and to go to such lengths as converting to Islam (a religion not known for its tolerant attitude toward gays or sex outside marriage) in an attempt to *cure* myself.

And so it was that in 1985 I found myself signing a marriage contract with a Palestinian Muslim from East Jerusalem whom I'd met while visiting Israel a few months earlier. I knew I loved him; however I also knew—even as I signed the contract—that I was making a terrible mistake in believing that this kind of love would give me anything but the remotest sense of satisfaction. Still, I persisted in trying to convince myself that it was *for the best,* that it was my only hope of ever having a child, and, given that my ex was a decent person, that I would eventually be able to forget about my attraction to women and concentrate on becoming an excellent mother and *acceptable* wife.

For the first few years it seemed as if I had made the right decision; we adopted one girl and then, thanks to *in vitro* fertilization, I gave birth to another. But still there were problems—big problems. Sex, for example, was a nightmare, something I endured rather than enjoyed, and something I tried to avoid at any cost, only giving in to my husband out of either pity or gratitude (but never desire). After all, he *had* helped me to become a mother despite being fully aware of my attraction to women, even adopting against the wishes of his family—and adopting, albeit unknowingly, a disabled child to boot. I will always be in his debt for that. (We later adopted a little boy.) But emotionally we were as far apart as any two human beings could be. In the second half of our marriage we hardly spoke, let alone slept together, and we limited our discussions to ones concerning the children.

People have asked me what it was like to be in a marriage devoid of any kind of physical or emotional closeness, especially when every part of me cried out to be with a woman. It was unbearable. Though my husband shared the same space and tried to maintain some semblance of *normality,* with each passing day we grew farther apart. So in the summer of 1999, when I was offered the chance to spend a few weeks in the States, it came as no surprise to either of us that I felt elated and relieved. For a few weeks at least, I would be spared from *pretending* things were OK. What I didn't realize, as the plane left Tel Aviv, was that by the time I returned I would have made a decision that would change the entire course of my life.

I'm still not sure what happened in the States. Perhaps it was my newfound sense of freedom, the lack of pressure, or simply the hours I spent alone contemplating my life, the choices I had made, and what the future held in store for me, but by the time I returned I knew that no matter how hard it would prove to be—on me, my ex, and my children—the marriage had to end. I also knew that my *fascination* with women was not a phase. I would never again be with a man. By denying my true sexual orientation, I was doing myself a great injustice and depriving myself of what I now consider one of the most basic human rights: the right to love the person of one's choice—regardless of sex—and to live with that person in peace and dignity.

Somewhat ironically, it was my ex who helped me find a temporary solution to my dilemma. The day after my return from the States, I quietly and as calmly as possible told him I wanted a divorce. I also told him the main reasons why, including that I could no longer ignore my being gay. His response was rather surprising at the time, but in retrospect somewhat predictable given his tendency to dismiss my feelings as something hardly worth consideration. He suggested I fulfill my desire to *be* with other women by spending time in one of the many lesbian chat rooms on the Internet. This solution ignored what I'd repeatedly told him, that my lesbian tendencies were only *one* of the reasons I wanted a divorce. Still, I listened to his suggestion and began to spend a lot of time *chatting* with other lesbians.

It wasn't always easy to hear the stories of these women I had never met. Many of them, like myself, had made the mistake of marrying only to realize their attractions to women were much more than a passing phase. But there were stories of triumph too, stories of married women who, having weighed all the pros and cons of finally abandoning the straight lifestyle, had eventually come out, separated, and then gone on to live exceptionally happy lives. These stories made me all the more determined to seek a divorce. They inspired me so much that in the autumn of 1999 I announced to my husband that, in the hope of discovering more about my true sexual identity, I was planning to attend the Open House, a lesbigay center in downtown West Jerusalem. I already knew what I needed to know: I was, by anyone's definition, a lesbian.

What was my husband's response? "Just be careful that nobody hears about it." As always, his prime concern was his image. As conservative as Arab society is, I couldn't really blame him. (Not until recently did I suspect that his *allowing* me to attend the center on a weekly basis was not due to love, kindness, or a genuine desire to help me through the most traumatic period of my life, but to a misguided belief that I would soon *tire* of my fascination with women and return to his waiting arms.) Either way I was glad to finally have the opportunity to mix with real live lesbians, and to confirm that my past brief relationships with women were far more significant than I had given them credit for. Now, armed with the support of a wonderful group of women friends at the center, I came out to myself.

Had I not lived in a society where being gay is still considered one of the worst crimes in existence, I might have thrown caution to the wind then and there and come out to everyone I cared about. Unfortunately I was all too aware that whereas my husband was happy enough to allow me to attend the center and even, should the opportunity arise, to take a female lover (assuming I was discreet), he was not about to agree to a divorce or grant me custody of the children without putting up a fight. This became even more apparent when I met Nili and it began to dawn on my husband that, despite the rumors spread by the straight community, lesbianism is not all about sex. The one thing he hadn't bargained for was actually happening—I was falling in love. And there was something else he hadn't bargained for: My lover, partly by being a woman, but mainly by being an exceptional woman, was succeeding where he had failed, most notably through providing me with the kind of emotional and physical satisfaction I had until then only been able to dream about. It wasn't like I had to tell him. He knew straight away. Much later he told me he had known it the very night I came home after my first date with Nili—that this relationship was going to be *different,* that we were one step closer to saying goodbye. But he wasn't going to make things easy for me. From that moment on he became obsessed with making my life as difficult as possible, taunting me, threatening me, and doing everything within his power to destroy my relationship with Nili. If not for Nili's love, support, patience, and wisdom, he probably would have succeeded.

Even today I don't know what it was that finally convinced my ex to admit defeat and let go. It could have been his listening in to the numerous nocturnal phone calls between Nili and me, many of which went on well into the early hours of the morning. (During these calls she repeatedly told me that she loved me, that I had a right to a life, that her being an Israeli Jew and I a married British Muslim with three children was no reason for us to part, that I could trust her, lean on her, and count on her to be there for me no matter what.) Or perhaps it was that finally, after years of walking around in a trance, I was beginning to display something akin to happiness—something he knew he couldn't give me. Or perhaps it was simply that I was suddenly empowered with a desire to *live* rather than merely *exist*. I slowly became more and more sure of myself, my needs, and of the path I was to take. In June 2000 my ex finally signed the divorce papers (but only after I threatened to come out to his family and ruin his reputation as a *man* if he didn't), thereby allowing me to take the children and move to West Jerusalem on the other side of town.

I should probably explain why it was necessary for me to move to Israeli West Jerusalem rather than remain in Arab East Jerusalem. To begin with, in spite of their geographical proximity, the two areas couldn't be more different, especially from a cultural point of view. For example, in the predominantly Muslim East Jerusalem, even the sight of a married heterosexual couple displaying any kind of affection in public is still considered unusual. But the sight of two men or two women holding hands or kissing would most likely result in bloodshed! And after spending so many years in the closet I simply wasn't prepared to hide any longer. In other words, feeling obliged to choose between all and nothing, I chose the former, which was clearly in West Jerusalem.

It's not as if I really had a choice. Had I remained in East Jerusalem, my every move would have been scrutinized not only by my ex-husband's family, but also by society as a whole. Living there as a foreigner was hard enough, but to live there as a divorced gay foreigner? Forget it. There was also no way that Nili, an Israeli, could have visited me in my home without my being branded a *traitor* by my less tolerant Palestinian neighbors. The idea of us living together openly was unthinkable, and neither of us wanted to conceal the nature of our relationship.

I have never met a lesbian in East Jerusalem, which does not surprise me. If a Palestinian girl or woman were to come out as a lesbian, whether she were Muslim or Christian, she would, at best, be rejected by her family and society. At worst—and this is no exaggeration—she would be killed by a male relative eager to protect the *family honor*. This is one of the main reasons why the only openly gay or lesbian Palestinians I have ever met live abroad. Of course, even in West Jerusalem, with its huge population of Orthodox Jews, being gay isn't easy. It is, however, much easier than on the other side of town. Today, even though the gay scene is nothing in comparison to that found in Tel Aviv, there exists a number of gay-friendly clubs, restaurants, and meeting places, such as my second home, the Open House, where gays can assemble and interact safely.

I have numerous reasons to be grateful to the Open House. First, it provided me with a safe haven, where I could let down my defenses and be myself. I still remember my first meeting; I was petrified, not only of being recognized as I entered the building, but also of being rejected by the women there, all of whom were Israeli and aware that I was married to a Palestinian. I couldn't have been more wrong, and even today I often wonder if I would have continued on my journey of self-discovery without the love and support I received there.

Second, I met Nili during one of the weekly meetings at the Open House. Our mutual attraction was undeniable; from the moment she entered the room she had me mesmerized. Everything about her fascinated me: her eyes, her mouth, her bone structure, her body language, her sense of humor. But more than anything else, what fascinated me was her nonconformist attitude—evident in the way she wore her hair in a ponytail regardless of whether it was a style favored within the community—and her total lack of respect for abiding by gay or straight norms. Was it love at first sight? Is there even such a thing? I'm not sure, but the chemistry between us was (and remains) incredibly powerful, so powerful, in fact, that only a few weeks later we knew we were in love.

Since meeting Nili I have come out to practically everyone who really matters to me: my children, my parents, and my closest friends. All of them responded positively to my announcement, even my father, whose views concerning homosexuality I knew all too well and with whom, since my early teenage years, I'd had an uneasy relationship. My father and I are very much alike inasmuch as we're both rather stubborn, have volatile tempers, and can sometimes be too blunt. This had created a rift between us I desperately wanted to heal. Therefore, not surprisingly, the idea of coming out to him scared me to death, and at first I avoided it. But I knew deep inside that until I confronted my fear and told him the truth, the joy I felt at finally coming out to myself wouldn't be complete. Therefore, with Nili's help (in addition to the encouragement of my "second mum," Nili's mother—who is surely one of the wisest and most compassionate women I know), I set about writing a letter that remained in my bag for almost two weeks before I plucked up the courage to send it. And when I did send it, it was with tears streaming down my face and a heavy heart. It truly felt like I was saying goodbye to my father, if not both parents, forever. Only my determination to do what was right gave me the strength to go through with it.

His response couldn't have been more surprising. Instead of the expected angry phone call or letter, there was nothing; and as the days turned into weeks I became increasingly convinced I would never hear from him again. The sadness I felt was unbearable, so unbearable that after a fortnight, halfway through a conversation with Nili about something totally unrelated, I suddenly jumped up and headed for the phone. "I'm going to call my father," I told Nili and, with her arms around me, I dialed the number.

At first the conversation was somewhat awkward, as if both of us needed to say something but didn't know where to start. Finally I took the lead and asked if he had received the letter. "I did," he said. "And I want you to know one thing. All we want is for you to be happy." At that very moment I began to truly appreciate the extent of my father's love for me. I also realized how terribly proud I was—of myself, of my father, and of being my father's daughter. And that pride will remain with me for the rest of my life.

As for my children, their reactions to hearing that mommy was gay were very surprising. My son was more concerned that Nili and I weren't married than he was that we're both women! I was, of course, very concerned that their father would tell them before I did, which is why, one night as I bent to kiss them good night, I told them. Fortunately, they had already met Nili and decided she was "cool," which made things a lot easier, especially as they had seen us be openly affectionate and, most probably, had come to their own conclusions. Still, the conversation was not without its more difficult moments. For example, although my 11-year-old daughter had no problem with my being "different" from most women and with my explanation as to why, she burst into tears when I nodded my head in response to her question, "But Mommy, does that mean you're gay?" She'd heard from several sources that according to Islam, being gay means going to hell. (I should mention that, to the best of my knowledge, there is nothing in Islam that directly condemns lesbianism, male homosexuality, and sex outside of marriage are entirely different matters.) Holding her close, I asked her if she thought God was smart and kind. "Of course," she replied. "Then tell me," I said, "how God could possibly send me to hell for loving someone as wonderful as Nili." It seemed to do the trick, and within seconds she was brushing away her tears. Then, just as I went to leave the room, she grabbed my hand and said something I will never forget: "You know what, Mommy? You're right, and I'm happy for you. It's been such a long time since we saw you smile, but these days you're always smiling and look so pretty, and now I know why. I love you, Mommy." Then she turned her head and fell asleep.

My daughter was right. These days, I *am* smiling. Nili has remained true to her word, even though our life together is by no means easy; my eldest daughter is physically and mentally disabled, while my other two are still enjoying the "benefits" of playing one divorced parent against the other. But she never complains and is always quick to convince me that things will get better. And you know what? They *are* getting better, if for no other reason than now, at last, I truly believe that—like everyone else—I have the right to live my life the way I choose and to love the person of my choice. Armed with that knowledge, I can take on the world and win, even if it involves something as simple as holding Nili's hand in public, wearing a NOBODY KNOWS I'M A LESBIAN pin, or riding down the road on bikes bearing pride stickers with Nili and the kids. It's been a long, long journey, but one that was definitely worth the fare.

A True Story...About Love

Sonia Furini

It was so long ago, yet not so long after all. It began at a crucial time in my life. I was 12 years old when I first realized my feelings about love and relationships. But there were so many other things happening: My parents were divorcing, we were moving to another city, I was starting junior high, and to make matters worse, I got my period. So I pushed my thoughts to the side and went on with my "normal" life.

The first time I kissed a girl, I knew. In hindsight, I should have embraced those feelings, but it was too confusing for me. Throughout high school and a tour in the military there were a few more instances of my exploration. I never treaded much past a kiss, fearful of what it might mean, who I would be to the world. And I was far too concerned with acceptance to venture further into that domain.

After one failed marriage and into my second one, I made a firm decision to take hold of the feelings of my youth. Up until then, my life revolved around church. I was thoroughly caught up with being a leader in the church, a Sunday school teacher, and a member on various church committees. To conservatives, I'm sure my life looked picture-perfect. But I was dying inside—dying to know and be loved by a woman.

Then there she was, walking in the church hallway to pick up her children. She left me totally rapt from the moment she walked past me, brushing against my shoulder as she went. She was the most beautiful creature I had ever seen. I wondered how I would ever approach her, how I could even bring up the subject? I struggled with a yearning to have her in my life.

As luck would have it, we ended up playing on the church

softball team together. She was an awesome shortstop, and I struggled in my attempts to be a good pitcher. I nudged my way into her life and we became fast friends.

I approached her with the question in an Instant Message: "Have you ever been attracted to women?" Her answer was no. I asked if she thought I was attractive. She answered that she thought I was a pretty lady, but to say I was attractive meant that she was attracted to me. So I left the questions alone, believing I had offended her, having thoroughly embarrassed myself.

But once again, as luck would have it, we were watching a movie at her house and she complained of an aching neck and back. I graciously accepted the opportunity to have my hands on her body. What started as reciprocal back rubs ended in me giving her a facial massage. After several minutes, she sat up abruptly. Once again, I felt I had offended her. The next day we discussed what had taken place, and I apologized. She accepted and explained that the reason she got up so quickly was because the feel of my hands on her face brought up strange feelings inside her. This was all the encouragement I needed.

That night I telephoned her. We talked and sighed and enjoyed each other for more than 12 hours. I rose the next day to go to work and she slept like a baby. Finally I could not hold myself back any longer, and I called her again. I was pleased to know that she was glad I had called. She was coming to my office to give me her first kiss. I was nervous. When she walked into my office three hours later, my heart was pounding. I still see her in my mind's eye—wearing brown jeans and a sweater, her hair and makeup done to perfection. She shut the door behind her and sat down. We smiled at each other, and I got up from my chair. I walked over to her, bent down, and offered her a soft peck on the lips. Then I returned to my seat. She looked at me quizzically, then simply said, "Oh, no!" as she rounded my desk. She stood me up and lip-locked me, sinking her tongue deeply and softly into my mouth. I was hooked, and so was she.

That evening I drove like a maniac to her home. We walked back to her bedroom, hungry for another taste of what we had had earlier in the day. She touched me, and I felt as though I would melt. I watched as she undressed me in front of the ceiling-high mirrors, enjoying seeing her hands on my skin. Again our mouths found each other, and we kissed deeply, passionately. She placed her hands on my ample breasts and then took my pink nipples into her mouth, sucking and tugging at them gently. I almost collapsed from sheer ecstasy.

I could stand it no longer, and I forced her back onto her bed. I tore her clothes off and stopped. I was amazed and awestruck by what was before me. Her body was perfect, *she* was perfect. I placed my body on top of hers, again kissing her. I slowly moved down her neck to her bare breasts and sighed under the feel of them in my mouth. Still, I moved lower until I found her mound of almost-black hair. My tongue went after her voraciously, savoring every taste of the sweet juices flowing from her. She was dripping wet, and I was glad to persist in lapping up every drop that I could possibly get. It was the most freeing and amazing moment in my life. I did not allow her to have her way with me that day. I made her wait until the next morning.

I left the door unlocked so that she could enter the house and find me in my bed. I was anxiously awaiting her arrival. We fell into each other's arms and once again delight filled the air around us. This time, she took control and pressed my body against the bed. She gently spread my legs and then buried her face in my auburn hair. The feel of her tongue against my innermost parts was overwhelming and before long I was climaxing, my legs tensing around her head, yet she feverishly continued to lick me, taking pleasure in her accomplishment. She laid her soft skin against mine and our bodies gave way to the satisfaction of the moment.

Our relationship continued much the same way through the months, full of surprises and wonderful sexual experiences. But it was during our first camping trip together that we realized for the first time in our lives that we were truly, deeply in love. We dreaded returning home, facing the reality of our individual and separate lives.

Within a short time, having separated from our husbands, we moved in together. We didn't realize the trials that our decisions would bring. Her husband fought for custody of her children. My husband was too worried that I would find out about his affair. After we had lived together 10 months, she moved out to avoid losing her children. I moved one week later, two doors down from her. This really distressed her soon-to-be ex-husband, because his original goal to keep us apart had failed. We joyously continued our relationship by sneaking over in the middle of the night for a "snack," or even spending the night with each other while our children were with their fathers.

My relationship with her was wonderful. I had never loved or been loved by someone so completely. She filled every void in my life and brought me great and wonderful joy. I would say to her, "You make me sparkle." And she would reply, "You've always sparkled." And finally, I would tell her the truth from my heart, "Not until your light shone on me."

I have always lived my life "out loud." But I've hidden my true self behind closed doors, afraid of losing my career, afraid of the wrong people finding out. After being laid off from my job with a Christian company, I've decided to hide no longer. I've decided to be who God intended me to be—a lesbian.

Scene 1: I'm Coming Out

Tonya D. Parker

I should have seen it coming when I became aroused by Sharon Stone in *Basic Instinct*. *It'll go away,* I thought. Even when I secretly tuned in to Skinemax movies on Friday nights, masturbating to girl-girl sex scenes, I'd tell myself, *It's no big deal. These feelings are natural. I'm in love with Kevin.* As a counselor, I normalized my growing attraction to women as much as possible, even when I began to fantasize about them when I made love with my husband. Fantasies are healthy, I'd rationalize. Even same-sex ones. I wasn't a lesbian, just open to a number of erotic experiences.

Therefore, it shouldn't have been a great shock when, at age 31, I fell in love with an actual, flesh-and-blood woman.

I had been married to Kevin for over five years; we had been together for 10. My tall, handsome, intelligent, successful black man. A preacher's kid. My Southern Baptist working-class family was so proud. I was the envy of many a sistah. Then along comes a woman. A white woman at that. One who had a girlfriend and did not return my love—at least in the romantic sense. *How the hell did I fall into such a mess?*

I met Kate playing softball. She was new in town and joined the team hoping to tap into the local community of lesbians. It was spring, a time of new life, new beginnings, and, apparently, new love. I just didn't know it at the time. Though there were no other out lesbians on the team, Kate and I hit it off—despite her wariness about my having played ball on a church team. We swapped jokes about our power-tripping coach. Our jokes led to further chats, and we found we had a lot in common. So much in fact that one night we talked after our game until two other games were done and the park lights were turned out on us. We shared interests in liberal politics, sports, healthy cooking, working with children. We had graduate degrees and similar experiences with family. We were both disillusioned by organized religion, and we even both had two holes in one ear, three in the other. Despite our racial, socioeconomic, and sexual-orientation differences, I had found my soul mate.

Kate and I also shared a dream of writing. We began to spend even more time together, collaborating on a children's book. Her partner, Lorrie, was supportive and encouraging. I got to know Lorrie better and was charmed by her intelligence, warmth, and generous spirit. I opened myself up to both of these women and allowed myself to slowly blossom with their love and acceptance.

I think what kept drawing me to Kate was her likeness to me. I felt she was a reflection of myself, in a fun-house mirror sort of way (after all, she was white, lesbian, and from a more affluent background). Though I had queer friends and coworkers, I had never been so close to a woman-loving woman as I was to Kate. I saw that, though she was a lesbian—from some Christians' standpoint, an abomination— she was a wonderful person. I loved being with her and Lorrie; the two of them were very good together. For the first time I became privy to a healthy, functional lesbian relationship, and I liked what I saw. I began to more fully question society's, Christianity's, my family's, and my own beliefs about homosexuality and life's possibilities for women.

But Kevin was no dummy. Though neither of us understood the scope of my feelings at the time, he knew on some level that Kate was a threat to our way of life. "Stay away from them," he'd say, referring to Kate and Lorrie. I thought he was crazy. Why should I avoid these women who made me feel so comfortable and so happy? Who was he to dictate who my friends would be?

Kevin wasn't the only person to notice my feelings for Kate. Several coworkers and a sister-in-law were all curious about the woman I couldn't stop talking about. I seemed to be the last to know. I was just so thrilled to finally have a friend that I could share so much with. It took me months to admit that my feelings went beyond sisterly love and friendship.

So there I was, married to a great guy, discovering I was in love with another woman and maybe a bit enamored with her relationship with her lover too. This love quadrangle left me feeling confused, scared and depressed. After all, I had a pretty good life. I was healthy, attractive, educated, employed, and married, and also a homeowner well on my way to buppiedom. This was not the time to rock the boat.

Nonetheless, I felt my life had capsized, and I began to slowly drown in a sea of confusion. Though I knew I could never be with Kate, it ceased to matter; I knew I had to live honestly and could not continue to be with Kevin, or any man. Now that I had finally opened the floodgates to my woman-loving feelings, there was no turning back, no settling for what society expected of me. But I knew this acceptance would affect my marriage as well as my family, career, friendships, and spiritual practice.

Since then, my life has played out like a strange movie full of complex characters, gut-wrenching drama, bizarre and unexpected comedy, and quite a danceable soundtrack (from "Shackles on My Feet" and "I'm Coming Out" to "I Will Survive" and "Independent Woman, Part I"). If somebody had assigned ratings, at times they might have marked my movie XXX, but mostly it's been PG. There have been times when I've wanted to shut down the production, or at least film retakes, but somehow I've filmed on. Now, three years after the first scene, I've thrown off my shackles, come out in full force, and survived to tell the tale of a finally independent woman's production.

I'll Be Seeing You

Rebecca Barnebey

I met her in April, but I knew she was coming long before then. The anticipation of her felt like a gentle tugging at my breast as a babe suckling in the night. I thought it was the company of women that would change my life. I had raised three sons with a loving male partner, but there was something missing. I often thought it was a daughter or missed time with other mothers in the neighborhood. When we had babies and infants we made time to drink tea together. Where had those days gone? I knew I was being called, but I had no idea I was to be led by one woman....

We traveled together across our state for 21 days in the company of other women who were also concerned about the fate of the planet and the health of our state and its inhabitants. We made our way on foot, by bicycle, and in canoes, meeting with other environmental activists, hearing firsthand of their work to improve the quality of life in their communities. Since I was a school nurse interested in respiratory health, my personal concern was to improve air quality.

One night halfway across the state, a storm blew our tents all night long. I lay awake listening, hearing, feeling, waiting. Something, someone was calling me, holding out a hand and bidding me to come. I was haunted that night by her presence, and I knew that our friendship was something that would be different from any I had ever known. Several nights later I spoke with an old friend who was also on the expedition, and we pondered the lack of physical contact we knew with our longtime male partners, debating whether we might ever find ourselves in love with another woman. As I look back, I think I knew the answer to that question the night of the storm. The last night of the trip I rolled my sleeping bag next to Hers, this amazing woman whose presence I had felt so intimately as the wind raged through our camp. We talked until early dawn. I wanted this night to last forever. I never wanted to sleep again, I just wanted to remain in her presence.

But the trip ended and we returned to our lives. We saw each other a couple of times and somehow the letters began. For close to a year we would write nearly every day, soul mates in search of each other. We wrote of our days, the books we read, the spider webs we avoided, our fourth grade teachers, our dreams, the birds we watched, our fathers, the bike rides we took, our understanding of life, and the simple meals we prepared for our families. With children, jobs, and husbands to juggle, it was difficult to see each other, but we found time for bike rides, some in my territory, others in hers. In her presence I could do things I had only dreamed of—ride hands-free, ride standing up, ride up relentless hills, ride at night with no fear, and ride through rain, sleet, and snow. We sat together in silence watching turtles, waterbugs, clouds, and melting snow. I felt as if we watched with the same eyes. I knew we had been twins in another life.

Our time together would take me to a completely different world, and then one of us would check her watch, and we'd race back to our other lives, singing, *I can't change how I'm living, but you can know who I am.*

We sat one night waiting for the train that would carry her across the river. There was a silence, a knowing, a yearning, and though it was unnamed we both felt the distance between us shrinking. I had once known something like this spiritual connection with my mother and then with my youngest son. We could communicate without words. But there was more. I could look out my window and know that she was looking out hers. I could watch the sunrise and see her gazing at the same sky. I could look at the full moon and feel it shining on her face.

It was a cold, rainy day in January. People asked why we were out on bikes in such weather, but cold and wet were never the same when I was with her. We parked our bikes and sat on a picnic table under a pavilion. It was as if the rain drew a curtain between the rest of the world and us. Her lips were the softest I'd ever felt; her tongue so tender. The touch of her fingertips on my face, like the caress of a newborn's tiny hand, carved a print I will carry forever. How strange that one, like myself, who has lived her life so tuned into words, books, and figures was to be led by the goddess incarnate to a completely new knowledge of myself. Touching her and feeling her touch was a way of knowing more of me than I ever knew existed. I was never more beautiful. I never felt so loved and I was never more creative in my expressive abilities. For the first time I understood why people had weddings. I wanted the whole world to know how much I loved her. I suddenly understood the scene at the end of *Like Water for Chocolate*. The passion I felt with her was enough to make life feel complete. It would be all right if our love were to consume us.

We sang Tracy Chapman's "The Promise": *If you wait for me, then I'll come to you.* But I didn't want to wait. I wanted to spend my days with her now. I wanted to ride my bike into the sunset with her and leave the safe and comfortable life of heterosexuality behind, and I made this very clear.

The last time I saw her we were parting in the middle of the giant bridge over the river that separated our lands. We had met here many times before. We didn't drift apart; our parting was abrupt. She said over the phone, "We can never see each other or talk to each other again!" I asked, "Never?" She said, "Yes, never," and that was it. In my mirror I initially saw a woman who didn't care whether or not she lived—it really wasn't worth being alive without her. I watched a giant truck approach my car in a pouring rainstorm and I thought, *It would be easier to be smashed on the highway than to find a way out of this sadness, this feeling of being torn from my twin.* I pulled over and asked myself, *What's happening to me?* I dreamt that I was locked in a large building that was being torched. I frantically tried every door and every window but a man stood at each one. In the dream, the panic drained out of me, and I accepted the coming inferno. I awoke knowing she had burned my letters and there would be no more between us.

There was to be no return to safe and comfortable for me; perhaps it has worked for her. I would move on knowing that nothing could ever take away my memories of her or what it felt like to be loved by her, to know her touch. I sing, *I'll be seeing you...* as I look back at my entire life.

It was a year before I allowed anyone to come near me again. I was shocked to feel my body respond to the touch of a sweet woman on a dance floor. This woman tried her best to reach me. We dated for several months. In the comfort of her arms I gained the strength to leave my husband and relocate to the land where I came of age. My family of origin, the women of my clan, have taken the time to listen to my story.

I am as different from them as I always was. For now, they don't understand me any better as a lesbian, but I am still daughter, stepdaughter, sister, and girl cousin, and I am cradled in their arms.

I have left a neighborhood that nourished me, my husband, and my sons for 29 years. There are many who don't understand my actions. How could I betray my husband? How could I leave my sons? How could I give up on the neighborhood? How could I desert them? Some people have questioned whether they know me or whether they ever knew me. I don't feel different, but I do feel more. I look more openly, listen more deeply, feel more freely, and live my life more simply than I could possibly do in a large East Coast city. I have carefully chosen the old friends I remain in touch with. For the most part these are women who have been more "my" friends and less "our" friends.

Telling my sons was the hardest part so far. I wanted my husband to be with me when I told them. Our boys were raised knowing their parents worked together as a team, and I didn't want a conversation this important to the rest of our five lives to happen without his presence. Each boy responded a bit differently. The oldest, who's currently considering a long-term commitment with his girlfriend, tried desperately to talk me out of my decision to leave the marriage. He argued that he understood the importance of same-sex "friends" but wanted our family to stay together. My second son was more straightforward and merely said that he knew this information could never change the fact that he has two parents who love him. The youngest was finishing his first year away at college. He credited the time he had spent watching TV for his ability to understand that relationships change and parents get divorced. But he also pointed out to us that it will be hard for him to see his parents with different partners.

My boys' father has made it clear that he will partner again. He wants to avoid all contact with me so he can "get on with his life." And this is not my choice; he has been my best friend for 37 years. I hold the thought that when he resolves his feelings of rejection and finds a way to forgive me for taking away his picture of our family, we can be friends again.

There are days when I believe I will never love again, that no other woman will ever reach as deeply into me as she did—my first lesbian lover.

Perhaps ours was love on a plane too great for mere mortals, although I never felt like a mere mortal when I was with her. She gave me a gift for which I can never be thankful enough. She allowed me to touch the goddess in her, and more importantly in me, and for this I am truly grateful. *I will remember you...weep not for the memories.*

Feminism, the Theory;
Lesbianism, the Practice

Terry Dunn

Times were different in the early 1980s. Some of us were arriving from two decades of trying to change the world, with a broad brush more than a personal one. The early "isms" had taken precedence in our lives—racism, classism, materialism, militarism, environmentalism. The more personal causes to fight for—sexism and discrimination against gays and lesbians—came later for us, in the Reagan years, oddly enough. Our private lives with men were in shambles. Arguments over the lesser value of our issues as women compared to men's issues, which were seen as more important, were not the least of our daily struggles. After 15 years of politicking, we still found ourselves in the position of the "housewife" on the domestic scene, the "woman behind the man" at the podium, the underpaid one in the work world, and the "one who got cheated on" in our personal relationships. We wanted equality and support in our personal lives, and the early 1980s offered it to us.

Somewhere out of the blue, or so we thought, a women's culture (read "lesbian culture") appeared before us, in particular me and about eight of my friends. We were living and working in a medium-size Midwestern city.

Two of us had met defending an abortion clinic. Two others had met at a demonstration against a Right to Life convention. Several others had met at a protest against a "head shop" store window display that presented dog-collared female mannequins chained to beds, smoking from hookahs.

We became sort of a group as we became better acquainted through a college philosophy class in feminist theory, a class where adults from the community were invited to participate. The teacher wanted students to meet activists, to see the different philosophical premises from which people take action represented by real-world people and events. Little did the teacher, or the participants, know that this class would serve as a lesbian incubator. The breakouts into small group discussions turned into consciousness-raising sessions.

The class affected people strongly. Some younger women became first-time feminists. Some women left abusive husbands or boyfriends in search of a more decent man. Our "group" of straight, longtime political activists gradually converted to the lesbian lifestyle, some right away, others a year or two later. In the late 1990s, four of us reflected upon our journeys into lesbianism. We were in town for a conference and met at a women's coffeehouse to catch up with each other about our lives. We were all at or approaching age 50.

Gradually we slipped into our coming-out stories, as lesbians often do. For us, it was also a reflection on the politics of an era.

Judy: You know, I have always thought how it was like a lesbian-feminist shooting star had zipped over our Midwestern city and zapped a bunch of us. I can name about 12 women myself who came out in the early '80s. I bet between us, we could name several dozen women who "entered the life" in Cincinnati in that time period. Don't you think?

Terry: Yep. I can think of quite a few. I remember thinking something like that myself, that our town underwent a sea change of sorts. It was amazing. But that kind of community feeling is gone now. I am glad to have been lucky enough to have lived through it. It was the best of times.

Judy: Yeah. Working in women's bookstores, playing softball on dyke teams, singing in a lesbian choir, writing for lesbian newspapers, coming out to our friends and coworkers, fighting for human rights ordinances. They were exciting times.

Nancy: Yep. I gradually replaced my buttons that said GIRL IS A 4-LETTER WORD—which isn't even necessary in 1998, thank heavens—and 59 CENTS FOR EVERY $1, and WOMEN FOR SOLAR ENERGY with A WOMAN WITHOUT A MAN IS LIKE A FISH WITHOUT A BICYCLE! Not that I stopped caring about het feminist issues—and I still proudly exhibit those buttons on the protest hat I wear at marches today—but lesbian politics and culture became my mantra.

Judy: Yeah. I remember the first time I saw that saying on a T-shirt…about the fish and the bicycle. I was intrigued. Here was this impressive, tall, confident woman walking across a parking lot in a desert national park, of all places—and all by herself, with a Great Dane—I thought she must be the Amazon incarnated; all by herself and not seeming to fear anything.

Was she really so blatantly saying she didn't need men? I have never forgotten that image. And I know it's the kind of self-possession and self-confidence that I saw in her that helped me consider a lesbian lifestyle for myself. That image of strength and not backing down or giving in, which I seemed always to be doing with men, was a huge lure for me to the lesbian world.

Pat: Yeah. A het friend—she was questioning her sexuality at the time—had asked me if I wanted to go to a lesbian concert, and I said, "Why would I want to go to a concert of theirs?" She said, "Well, why not? It'd be interesting." And I replied, "Well, I guess it couldn't hurt." And I really liked Holly Near—her politics and her strong, luscious voice.

I knew her from my anti-Vietnam days, and I owned every last one of her political records. I had heard that she had gone "over to the fold," so to speak, and I'd been sorry to hear that. It seemed every woman I knew at that time was "going that way." I was feeling left out.

Judy: Yeah, I remember feeling left out too. All my straight women friends were giving up on men. I was a long-time holdout, though. Hoping that the sensitive New Age guy that I was seeing would just change a few more things and wind up OK to be with.

Terry: Nancy, so when do *you* feel you really came out—to yourself, that is?

Nancy: Well, I had left my "lefty" boyfriend of five years one day because I saw I just couldn't count on him to stand behind me when the chips were down. Only women were supporting each other in that demonstration against the head shop window. You remember that? He and I got into the worst fight about pornography. I said it objectified women and he said it helped men release their tensions, or some such nonsense.

Terry: Yeah, I remember that demonstration. It was yucky.

Nancy: Well, after the breakup, I spent at least a year checking out lesbian concerts, all those Olivia Records musicians that were criss-crossing the country. And I'd been volunteering at the women's bookstore—had even been their very first volunteer—the straight woman! And I'd been reading and keeping my ears open to learn about this lesbian world. Well, one day another volunteer—but a dyke—asked me if was I calling myself a lesbian yet. Well, put bluntly like that, and feeling on the spot and like an interloper if I didn't say yes, I said, "I guess I *am* one." It was a weak response verbally, but powerful to my self-identity after that moment. I remember my pounding heart right after I answered her and the sweat on my face. Sheesh. It was something!

Terry: So you didn't come out through a love affair?

Nancy: No, I didn't. I was a political lesbian feminist. And, you know, it makes all kinds of sense to me that a political declaration would be a crucial moment for me. Of course, there are lots of "coming outs" in one's life, but that was the first one. The second one would probably be the time I first had sex with a woman. I remember feeling like I had to pass *that* test before I could call myself a lesbian.

And I passed. A friend of mine showed me the ropes, so to speak, the physical part of "doing it." And though those breasts felt strange to me, I figured I'd get used to them. And my friend told me I did "just fine." Ha! It's funny when I think back on it now. How methodically and intellectually I approached this decision. Pat, let's hear your story.

Pat: Well, that Holly Near concert I mentioned.... You know, I was *really* put off by the butches in the crowd. I couldn't understand why they dressed like they did and walked tough like they did. I saw them as phony. I couldn't relate to them—and since I wasn't one of *them,* this lesbian world couldn't ever be a world *I* could ever claim. Plus, I was a jazz lover, and women's music was so folksy. Though I loved Holly Near, she was the exception to my musical interests. I would allow an exception or two, but I wasn't about to give up a 20-year refined musical taste just to fit in.

So it was a year later, and Holly came back to town. By this time I had discovered a women's jazz group called Alive!, and a jazz duo, and a few other bluesy-jazzy artists, so I wasn't so alienated from the women's music scene. And by then, I had adjusted to the butch type of lesbian—having found a few that I really liked personally helped me overcome my initial aversion. And by then I was part of a women's production company too. We'd been bringing to town different lesbian musicians, comedians, and choral groups. So when Holly came back to town, this time I was ready to be deeply changed.

Holly and her accompanist stayed at my apartment while they were contracted here. After her concert, Holly, her pianist, and three of us production company members sat in a car for hours just talking about relationships, coming out, oppression of gays and lesbians, and fun topics too.

When that conversation was over, I told a friend of mine

that very night that if a person like Holly could be a lesbian, then I could too. That was a crucial few hours for me. That's all I needed—someone I could strongly identify with, and of course, all that preparation work of the year before—getting used to this different world.

Terry: So you didn't come out through a love affair either?

Pat: No, I didn't. After that night, though, I was free to find someone, which I did in a couple months.

Terry: It took me several years to fall in love with a woman. I too came out through the culture, not through a specific attraction to someone. I liked the self-confidence I saw in the lesbians I met on the softball team, in the women's choir, and at other places in the community. I was well aware of having joined a community. I worried at first that a community of women wouldn't be diverse enough. But I found out to the contrary. There's every stripe of politics, styles, interests, and work choices that you find in the straight community—but of course, fewer people to find to fall in love with. Nevertheless, I saw that there would be different niches I could create friends in—even in this smaller community. There was an inverse relationship in my life at that time. Men were increasingly less attractive as lesbians became more attractive. And lesbians became more attractive as they became more of a possibility for me, by which I mean that as I became more comfortable with the idea of "being a lesbian," lesbians became more attractive. Many of them seemed so self-determined and so talented. Do you remember the Michigan Womyn's Music Festival—how in the early years we used to talk all the time about how great it was that women built it every year, without men's help. Built it physically, as well as organizing the whole big event. Built the stages, the sound system—for this crowd of hundreds, and later, thousands. We were all amazed at ourselves, at our abilities. Today we think nothing about women's abilities to hammer, dig deep ditches, do electrical wiring, drive big trucks, be musicians, and so on. But back then we were still proving these things to ourselves. Only later did we prove it to society at large.

Pat: What's the part of actually falling in love with someone then?

Terry: Well, like I said, it took several years to fall head over heels for someone. And it just felt so natural by then. I knew the lesbian world, was comfortable in it, had claimed it, so to speak, and when Barb appeared on the scene everything just fell into place. I had my new world. And now I had the lover piece that had been missing for a while. It was a great sense of completion to finally find her.

Pat: So none of us actually came to lesbianism the way "born lesbians" do—you know, from the cradle. We chose it after a life of trying men and failing, and then the women's culture came along and we had an option, finally. Would any of you ever go back to men?

Nancy: *No!* I still may not have found the dream woman of my life, but for me, it may just be OK to have girlfriends for as long as they last and then just wait for the next one. I feel like a flower child, like living in the moment is the best thing—and if this year it's Susie, and next year it's Mary...well, that just might be my own makeup. And I've decided that that scenario is just fine with me. I get something out of every relationship and that's cool.

Terry: Barb and I are in it till death do us part, I'm pretty sure. Though you can never be absolutely sure, I feel we are getting closer to each other all the time. It's great.

Judy: This lesbian thing is my thing. It took a long while to get to it, but I feel so much freer to achieve anything I want to achieve. I have such great support from my women friends that I feel I can really do just about anything I set my mind to. That's not something one would give up lightly. I see younger women today pretty much feeling that very confidence from the outset, and I think that if that is our legacy to the younger generation, great. It was quite a struggle for us to get to that point—but it was an exciting time, they were exciting struggles, and we felt they had great significance, those struggles. Today I still think they had momentous significance.

My married straight friends are still being put down by their husbands in that same cruel, obnoxious, supercilious way that I remember. It pains me to see them put up with it. Many men have still not changed. I would never walk back into the snake pit, now that I'm liberated.

Nancy: You know, we've lived through interesting times and grabbed the bull by the horns. And I think we're all the richer for it.

Terry: Yeah, we're the lesbians who some lesbians say can't exist. Who says there are no such women as political lesbians? We're them, aren't we?

Pat: Yep. We are. We do exist.

Snapshots

A Deeper Shade of Gray

duana r. anderson

Fingers of gray light crept through the darkness outside, the lush decay of vegetation rising within the sultry fog from rain-slicked asphalt and clinging to the edges of the patio door, stealing up the glass, sheathing the world in eternal twilight for yet another day. It had been two weeks since I'd stepped off the plane to meet Heidi, and I had yet to see the sun.

Vancouver was as dark and damp and mysterious as the ocean that bordered it. It was a netherworld, unchanging, stuck forever between illusions and reality, neither here nor there. Or perhaps it was only I who was in that state of flux and didn't realize that the world was moving past me in subtle stealth.

I stirred, swimming through layers of postintoxicated sleep. Stale cigarette smoke clung to my hair, and my tongue was woolly and sour. Heidi lay sleeping by my side, curled up like a shell. Her long, dark lashes feathered her cheeks, her small fists tucked under her elfish chin, her lips parted. I could see the inside pink of her mouth and I wanted so badly to probe that wet darkness with my tongue. I thought about last night and how I had tasted all of her—every mucous membrane, every saltwater morsel, all the dark damp secrets she hid within her folds.

God—was that last night? Last night! I turned over on my back, my arms behind my head, and stared at the foil stars stuck onto the black ceiling. Tie-dyed purple swirling cloth enveloped the bed like ether. The Indian cotton swayed and reminded me of a woman's hips. The smell of incense— patchouli and sandalwood—mingled with the ripe odor of sex and sweat. I felt as though I were falling up into the ceiling, into a spiral galaxy that spun around and around like a giant vortex about to swallow me.

I squeezed my eyes tight to fight back tears. What had I done? Scenes flashed behind my lids. Drinking warm, red wine and kissing warm, red lips. Soft woman-skin that smelled of beach and driftwood and rain. Drunk on passion, on the mysteries of female flesh. Had I really done all that? It felt like a faraway dream and the more I tried to think about last night, about the texture of her skin and the mewling sounds she made when she came, the more I wanted to forget. I rolled onto my belly and smothered my face into the pillow but could not escape the scent of sex and the ghosts of evenings past.

***

The afternoon was fresh from a sprinkling of rain, and overhead the clouds moved like an underwater current. Heidi and I had spent the day drifting through Gastown, finding treasures in secondhand stores that smelled of body odor and the essence oils they sold in strange little bottles, trying on their blast-from-the-past garments, haggling with merchants. We passed junkies bumming change and kids on skateboards, musicians playing bongo drums, guitars, and saxophones. We passed by a merry-go-round and she stopped so I could take a picture of her in front of it. She looked so childlike with her impish grin and sparkling eyes, her poet's hat tilted upon her head, strands of baby-fine hair clinging to her rosy cheeks.

My feet ached as I sat down at an outside café and put on a new pair of thick-soled leather sandals that I had just bought from a nearby leather store. We ordered hummus with Lebanese bread warmed in hot oil and spices and drank bottles of Greek beer. Our conversation was lighthearted as we remembered silly things about the past, the friends we used to hang around with, and the twins we used to date. We watched the people passing by. The afternoon turned quickly to twilight. As we left I threw my old runners into a nearby garbage can. Before we turned the corner I saw a young guy without shoes on fish them out, and a deep ache filled my heart. It was such a cruel, cruel world. What right did I have to be so oblivious to it?

The gray was more obscured than ever. It had a sort of dreamlike quality to it, and I felt as if I'd fallen through the cracks in the sidewalk to be reborn into a world where reality was just out of reach. Subtle things like the way the light swayed from the street lamps yet didn't quite illuminate anything, the earthy green smell that blossomed with the darkness and filled each breath. It was an urban jungle with predators, hookers, and junkies out prowling the streets, and all we have to protect us was our youthful idealism and our belief that nothing could hurt us.

We staggered into the party carrying half a bottle of Moody Blue in a paper bag. The music was loud, throbbing deeply, the air thick with blue incense smoke and sweat. It hit me like a sweltering rainforest. My vision was liquid, as the candles rippled shadows up the walls.

Heidi was lost in the throng almost immediately. I was content to lean against the living room wall, slugging back mouthfuls of the cheap wine, observing everything through my long, camouflage bangs. The room swarmed with young flesh posing for various provocative dramas. My sight drifted, hesitated, then drifted again. I watched a guy in a white T-shirt neck with a dark-haired chick on the couch. His mouth was possessive, hungry. The girl moaned, throwing back her head, throat outstretched. Such a nice long throat. Pale moon skin. Her dark hair splayed out on the arm of the sofa. Her eyes were dewdrops that reflected the intensity of her desire.

Then she saw me, my eyes staring, even from behind my camouflage bangs, and I felt the sudden shock of humiliation.

Heat stained my cheeks. She pulled her lover up by the hair and whispered something in his ear. He turned around and that's when I saw his breasts swelling the front of his white T-shirt. "He" was a "she." A dyke. Suddenly I saw the room and all the people in it as if for the first time. They were all women. Women with muscles and tattoos and body hair. Women who loved women—intimately. I had stepped into a lair.

A jolt shot through my pussy. The room swelled and breathed, suddenly much hotter than before—much darker and ponderous. The pounding that echoed in my ears was my own heart pumping against my chest, drowning out the words to Janis Joplin's "Summertime." I had never been the voyeur to eroticism between two women. Sure, I had experimented as a young girl with other girls, playing house, practicing kissing, groping underdeveloped breasts, show-and-tell twats—but this was entirely different. This was adult. This was real. I found it as fascinating as I did frightening. Deep inside of me I felt a fracture opening—something was shattered, and something new reborn from the broken pieces. A new entity borne of lust, of sexual forbiddenness, of truth perhaps? I had simply never before considered that I might have been lesbian or bisexual. I had spent the past 18 years in naïveté, isolated from reality by my own preconceived notions of who I was. And in the blink of a waxing eyeball, that identity was completely annihilated. I watched them, unable to look away. The dyke with the white T-shirt smiled back at me, then turned around to her girlfriend. Her hand slid under the girl's halter top, exposing the underswell of her breast. She began to fondle the soft flesh, working it like clay, stretching the nipple out until it hardened. Her head bent down and she sucked and licked at the brown thimble of flesh until it strained toward her. The girl arched up and pressed hard against the dyke's mouth. She was long and lithe like a cat. An ache throbbed deep in my pussy. I pressed the flat of my hand against that pulse, trying to push it back inside. No use. This newly awakened sexuality was not going to leave me so soon. It would have been easier to forget how to breathe.

A pair of hands sprang from behind me, shielding my eyes. I froze, sucking in a quick breath. "Hey there!" whispered Heidi's voice from the darkness. "You're beautiful when you blush."

I turned around to face her, blushing even deeper. "Jesus, you freaked me right out!"

"Groovy party, eh?" she said, taking a long draw on a joint.

"Fucking trippy!" I laughed awkwardly. I felt completely naked, as if I had been caught masturbating. She placed the joint heater into her mouth and then blew me a supertoke. I inhaled the smoke tasting of damp basements full of hydroponics equipment, artificial lights and mildew. Our eyes locked and our mouths pressed together for a second before she pulled away. I held the smoke deep within my lungs until my head fogged up. My eyes glossed over as the room wavered like rain blurring a windowpane. I wanted to snuggle into the soft, fuzzy corners of the room.

"Good weed..." I choked out. Heidi leaned against me and laughed, her hot breath kissing my neck. The room tilted ever so slightly and I felt the clumsy sway of the ocean beneath my feet, the tide tugging at my toes. I wrapped my arm around her shoulder and fell against her. Mmm...melting saltwater kisses, her curves hugging my own.

"Let's go home," she whispered, her soft mouth tickling my ear.

We walked arm and arm, swaying drunkenly. The bottle of wine passed from lip to lip, and I swore I could taste her upon it. We whispered, telling secrets, giggling like kids, about the uncertainty of the universe, how it went on and on forever, like a giant spiral into eternity. I rested my face against her neck and was curiously aware of the warmth of her flesh and throbbing pulse. Her hair intoxicated me completely. She wrapped her small hand around my waist and led me blindly through the deep gray shadows.

Heidi lit candles around the room as I undressed and flopped onto the futon in my undershirt. The soft down-filled mattress embraced me. I closed my eyes and listened to the lilt of a flute cascading from her CD player and floated on a cloud of placid stillness. It was Heidi's favorite CD, and she had told me earlier how it was a recording of a single flute in an empty cathedral. The music billowed in the small room, brushing against my skin. It felt soft as a warm current swelling over me. I pictured the flutist, an elfish woman with fine sandy-blond hair, hair like Heidi's, sitting cross-legged in the forest. Beams of sunlight slanted down through the trees that arched above her in a leafy dome. The air was thick as moss.

The weight of the mattress shifted as Heidi lay down beside me. I could smell her, feel the heat from her body. Her fingers brushed the hair from my forehead and her lips pressed against my cheek. I curled my face toward hers and sought out her mouth with my own. Our kiss was hesitant and gentle, testing the waters. Her mouth was so warm and soft, so unlike the crushing hunger of a man's. Our lips parted and I probed her smooth inside flesh with my tongue. My hand wove into her hair as she pressed her tender body to me so that I could feel the groove of her body fitting into my own curves. Suddenly, I yearned to touch her everywhere—to explore the forbidden fruits of her femininity.

Our shirts were lost in the sea of wet kisses, probing hands and fingers, soft thighs, grazing fingernails. Her nipples were puffy and filled my mouth, tasting sweet as ambrosia. She writhed beneath me, pressing close, legs tangled, bodies moist with sweat. Her moans were hot breathy whispers, barely audible. I enjoyed the feel of her small hands sliding over my skin, weighing the fullness of my breasts, tickling the back of my neck, probing between my thighs. The tip of my tongue tingled with her salty taste. I was on the threshold of a whole new pleasure.

Her pussy opened up to me, soft and pink and wet like dessert. I sucked and tongued the warm crevasse, eating her, drinking her, smearing my face with her passion fruit. The more she squirmed and pressed against me, the more delirious I became, the more hungry and bold. Her moans were long, drawn out like the whine of a violin. Her fingers dug into my scalp, pulled at my roots. My breasts were slick with sweat. She pressed my head hard against her, her body stiffened, shuddered, then her legs crushed around me and she let out a breath, half-moan, half-sigh. I gasped for air, but all I could smell was her, damp and lush like a spring rain.

For the longest time I lay cradled against her thigh, licking her cream. Sometime during the night I crawled into her arms and fell asleep, content and newborn.

Heidi shifted beside me and my thoughts drifted back to the morning haze that stretched gray fingers through the gauzy curtains. I turned and looked at her for a long time, watching her sleep. Confusion swirled inside me. This was too new to me.

Still, I knew I wanted to make love to Heidi again. Right then and there. I also knew I couldn't. Not now—not ever. The fissure deep inside me had opened wide, spilling out my emotions in a furious deluge. Nothing made sense anymore. Everything I had ever known seemed wickedly distorted now, like a cracked mirror reflecting a fractured image of something that had never existed before. I was forever changed. It scared the hell out of me.

Again I felt that terrible sense of panic, and more than anything else I wanted to throw up. As if by purging all the wickedness inside of me I could make everything all right again. I rolled over and quietly got up out of bed. Outside it had turned a deeper shade of gray.

The glass door swooshed closed behind me. I stood for a moment, my army duffel slung over one shoulder, trying to gain my bearings. Strangers rushed around me, some to catch their flights, some to meet other strangers, men in wrinkled business suits with carry-on bags, plastic voices calling departure times over the loud speakers, faces looking as lost and forlorn as I was certain mine did. My flight to Halifax would be arriving at Level C in 20 minutes. I had purchased a standby ticket half an hour earlier over Heidi's phone with my mother's credit card. I thought about the quick note I had scribbled and left on her bedside table with regret—how she would awaken and find me gone. I hadn't wanted to leave her like that. I hadn't wanted to leave her at all. But I didn't have the courage to face her just then. I didn't have the courage to face myself.

She was probably awake right now. A part of me longed to run back out that door and fall into her arms. Yet another part of me felt angry and betrayed.

The universe was spinning around me at that moment and all I could do was stand there and stare at the chaos. I took a deep breath, squeezed my eyelids tight to fight back my tears, and walked toward the escalator before I had a chance to change my mind. Later on the plane, I drank until I was numb, and it wasn't until years later that I finally stopped and accepted the truth of who and what I really was.

Dinner With a Friend

Karen Saginor

It's the candle's light
on the silver forks
and the wine glasses
on which I fix my concentration,
turning over the words I would use
to complete the rest of the story
now that I've started it.

You've found out part of it,
you noticed, you asked.
I don't want to be dishonest,
but what will you think, what will you say?
You don't know that I write poems to women
and I can't tell you,
I haven't got that courage.

Giving New Meaning to "Lesbian Visibility"

Tzivia Gover

For my partner and me, the invitation to my cousin's wedding—the hand-calligraphed envelope, the wisp of tissue paper like a veil over the gilt-edged card, and the phrase "Black Tie Optional"—all suggested discomfort.

It's never easy for a lesbian couple to show up at a family wedding. Although I must admit, for me it's easier than for most. For example, our invitation was correctly addressed to Ms. Gover and Ms. Swain, and I knew that both of our names would be lettered on a single place card, just as it would be for my married relatives. I didn't have to worry that we'd be made altogether invisible, as so many others in our position might be. But liberated and liberal though my family is, we're still talking wedding—a bacchanalian tribute to boy-girl pairing—and a pair of girls thrown into the mix always causes some level of anxiety on one side or the other, usually both.

The first thing we did to prepare was to shop for clothes. My partner and I have a bargain-basement budget, but we knew this wouldn't be a labels-for-less crowd. So in an effort to put the best foot forward on behalf of our minority group, we marched off to an upscale department store, the likes of which I haven't entered since I bid farewell to Long Island's Miracle Mile some 18 years ago.

I wouldn't exactly call myself a lipstick lesbian, although the only item of makeup I own happens to be a tube of lipstick. Nonetheless, I'm comfortable in a skirt and heels. My partner, on the other hand, has worn a dress only once in her adult life.

We were in bed one afternoon when the doorbell rang. She reached for the closest garment at hand and presented herself to the UPS man wearing my knee-length jumper.

So for the wedding I would wear a green silk dress, and she would shop for a suit. Thus, we found ourselves in this classy department store, arguing over whether we'd have more luck in the men's or women's department. We chose women's. And after finally convincing a saleswoman that Chris really would not consider any of the skirts she foisted upon us, we found a tailored brown pantsuit that did the job and did it quite splendidly. We paid and took the suit, swathed in a crisp white garment bag, out to the parking lot. I noted that our car could probably be traded in for a little less than we had spent on the suit.

On the day of the wedding, lacking blush or foundation, we first hit the beach to get tanned. This side trip meant that we arrived at the hotel, where the wedding was about to take place and where we had rented a room for the night, just a half-hour before show time. Chris ducked into the shower, shook out her hair, and proceeded to slip the garment bag off her new suit. I was applying my makeup—that is, my lipstick—when I heard a low, desperate groan from just beyond the bathroom door. I came out to find that the sales clerk had neglected to remove the plastic ink tag from the suit. This is a security device designed so that thieves can't leave the store without setting off an alarm, and if they do, they can't wear the item without having to display a chunky white button filled with black ink. Chris immediately grabbed her pocketknife, ready to saw off the offending item. "Stop!" I yelled. "It'll spray on everything, including the suit!"

We had exactly 20 minutes until the wedding. "They must have another branch of this department store in this town. We'll bring the suit and have them remove the tag." "Unless it's next door, we won't have time," Chris complained. I grabbed the phone book and at exactly 15 minutes to the hour I was spinning our tale of woe to an unruffled sales-woman. "Well," she said coolly, "if you can get down here before we close in 15 minutes, we can have that removed for you." "But," I hissed, "we have to be at my cousin's wedding in 15 minutes." She gave us directions from the hotel to the store. "How long a drive will that be?" "About 15 minutes," she said. I dropped the phone, grabbed the car keys, and, standing in my slip, heels, and lipstick, I summoned Chris. "Let's go," I said, one hand on the doorknob.

"This is insane," Chris said, stating the obvious. "We won't make it to the wedding in time, and there's no guar-antee we'll even make it to the store before they close." What to do? We had driven to the hotel wearing shorts and had packed jeans for the trip home. "Put on the suit," I said. Maybe the jacket will cover the tag." No such luck, the ink tag was located on the pants, mid-thigh. Of course Chris doesn't carry a purse, which could have been used to cam-ouflage the tag. She could fold the jacket over her arm and cover the tag, but that would be too casual for a wedding where the men were wearing tuxedos and the women gowns. "Forget it," she said, still looking drop-dead gor-geous despite the tag. "Let's go." I threw on my dress and positioned myself at her right elbow. If we matched our strides, my leg would block the ink tag from sight. More or less. As soon as we stepped out of our room, a man paused, nodded toward the tag, and raised his eyebrows as if to say, "Forget something?" "Oh, that," Chris said, smoothly. "It's an electronic tracking device. I'm on parole." The man looked her up and down and walked quickly away. Next, a woman in black silk, who was hurrying toward the wed-ding, touched Chris's shoulder. "You have a tag on your pants," she whispered discreetly.

"You don't think we could have paid for these clothes, do you?" Chris asked.

The woman backed away. "Sorry," she said, tottering on

her heels. "I just thought maybe they forgot to remove it at the store."

"At least they're not gawking at us because we're gay," I said as she retreated. We made it to the room where the wedding was about to begin. We were by now quite late, and the assembled guests were anxious to see the bride walk down the aisle. We scanned the room but could see no unoccupied seats. Finally, I saw two together. In the second row, center. "Come on," I said, "no one will notice." So I led Chris down the aisle. Heads turned. When I peeked over my shoulder I saw that well-manicured fingers pointed too. People didn't hide their smirks. They noticed.

We took our seats. "So much for blending in," Chris said. My cousin was gracious, although she did hesitate before Chris gave her a congratulatory hug, asking first if she was sure the tag wouldn't explode. A fair enough question, as she still had hours to go in that white silk dress. Now the wedding is over; the bride and groom have returned from their honeymoon. And we have our memories: a place card with both our names; the photograph in which I'm clinging to Chris's side to cover the ink tag; and our credit card receipt, on which is posted a very generous discount from the offending department store. Most of all, we have the satisfaction of knowing that if it's true that silence and invisibility are a form of death, and if the corollary that visibility is a way of affirming our lives is also true, then my partner and I have done our bit this year. And we didn't even attend any marches.

To Emma Lynn

Pandora Nu

She looks at me through lover's eyes.
She sees me though I try to hide
this side, my sexuality.
My family is more Chinese
than relatives still in Taiwan.
They've crystallized Confucian bonds,
not growing old with changing times;
their homeland has now modernized.
When my gay cousin first came out
to his *fumuqin,* they remained proud
as long as he still had his job.

Sometimes at night I cry. My love
soothes me with her hands, her kiss, her
total honesty. She says first
that who I am is for me to
be. Then, she says that I can choose
to free myself from guilt. To live.
Don't call. Don't write. Don't cave. Don't give
my life to them. Although I know
she's right, I'm still afraid to show
the world the truth of who I am.
I hope someday I will, my Em.

Snow
Tea Benduhn

As soon as I arrived in Winder, Ga., my orange 1972 VW Beetle promptly broke down: some sort of engine exhaustion. I puttered into the driveway, and Harold (my car) gave a last sputter and cough, then the death rattle wheeze. Since this was a small town pretty far from anywhere reasonable, and also a holiday weekend, there would be nothing we could do. I hopped out of Harold, and my brother, Jason, was immediately there to greet me.

"You look like a fuckin' dyke," he said.

"Surprise," I said.

"Shut up, punk," he said. "What's up with this shit anyway? Head all shaved and shit, combat boots. You either joined the army or the legions of lesbian cliché-ville."

"So what if I have?" I shrugged.

"Yeah, right." He circled around behind me. Inspect the sister. "And what's that? A tattoo?" He curled up his top lip as he looked at the back of my head.

I raised my eyebrows. "Duh."

"Cool." He shrugged, stepped back and leaned against an invisible wall. Mr. I-can-handle-anything-I'm-hip. "What's it of?"

"A fish." Like he couldn't see.

His eyes shined a little with admiration and smirking laughter. "Whatev." Kicked the hubcap of my car. "Piece of shit."

"Hey," I said, "it may be a piece of shit, but it's still *my* car."

"Freak," he muttered under his breath.

I grabbed my backpack and headed inside, swinging the

screen door with a little too much force. I forgot about that hinge. Dad must not have gotten around to fixing it yet.

And all Dad did when I got inside was chuckle lightly and say, "Heh-heh, cool." Then he nodded to the rhythm of that beat in his head. "Allllll-riiight. Welcome home, kiddo."

Jason came around to the kitchen. Not that the living room is far from the kitchen in my dad's trailer. He lit up a cigarette. "Hey, remember Karen Simonson?"

My stomach leaped a little and curled in on itself. "Yeah." She had been a year behind me in high school. Popular. Exactly the kind of girl I'd hated. Pretty, long brown hair, big eyes, strong legs. Everyone wanted to either be her friend or sleep with her.

"What about her?"

"I'm dating her."

"Yeah, right."

"No, seriously, I am."

"How did that happen?"

"She works at the Waffle House." He grinned.

So apparently he went to the Waffle House every day for his lunch break from his job cutting down dead trees. "I hadn't seen her since high school," he said. "Must've been four years"—he's older than me—"and when I saw her I was like, damn! That girl is fine. She looks like a deer with those strong, thin legs."

Like she would be good at dodging through a thicket of trees and making her way through the woods, out to the street full of headlights, I thought.

"She's got that hair the color of coffee," he continued. "Her eyes are like Hershey's Kisses, and her skin is like satin. Like, she looks like a French chick or something."

"Yeah," I said, "I know what she looks like."

"So when she asked 'What'll it be?' I thought I'd be original and say, 'I'd like a cup of coffee, a bowl of cheese grits, and your number.' She scribbled away on the order pad, handed me the ticket, and her number was on it."

It took him a few days to get up the nerve to call her, he said. But after he did, they spent every weekend together. They talked about stuff they had in common: parents who were either dead or had gone to jail, how they hated Winder and wanted to get out, and their disappointment in their siblings for leaving. For instance, Jason thinks I'm a snob for heading off to Greensboro to become "politically correct" and to suck out all the fun from jokes.

Meanwhile, Dad had other interests.

"How are you going to get back to school if it snows?" he asked during Thanksgiving dinner.

"It's not going to snow," I said.

"It might snow." He was pacing in front of the TV with his arms crossed, tugging at his mustache.

"I'll take a bus."

"You can't take a bus if it snows," he said. "There's nothing you can do if there's ice."

"I'll drive you," Jason said. "If it gets too bad, we can pull over."

"Then what?" Dad asked. "People freeze to death in their cars."

"Dad," Jason's voice was firm, as if talking to a child, "it's not going to snow so bad that we can't pull over at a reasonable place. It isn't like it's going to blizzard suddenly in the middle of South Carolina, for Chrissake."

Dad pulled on his mustache some more. He exhaled heavily through his nose, snorting like a horse. "Where would you pull over?"

"Well, Dad," Jason said, "that would depend on where we were at the time, wouldn't it?"

"I don't know," Dad said. "I don't like it. Doesn't look good." He started pacing again, picking up speed along the worn carpet. "It could snow, and you would be stranded somewhere in the mountains, and no one would save you."

He detached his fingers from his mustache. "I couldn't drive up there. I'd never find you." The pacing ensued.

"I'm not expecting you to find us," Jason said. "How the hell else do you think she's going to get back to school?"

"She'll just have to wait until after it isn't snowing."

"It isn't snowing *now*."

And that settled it. Another win for Jason. But meanwhile, really. As if I'd be expected to stay in a trailer in Winder with my dad and overgrown brother of all places. What's worse? Death by mountain or the slow suffocation of a rural Georgia town? Either way I'd be screwed.

Friday night, Jason took me with him to Karen's house. I'd rather not have gone, but it was better than staying home with Dad.

"Hi," Karen smiled when she opened the door. Jason kissed her forehead. She pulled away. He pushed past her into the house. She ignored him, kept looking at me. "I'm so glad to see you again after all this time!" We stood on either side of the open front door for a few moments, our cheeks hot, laughing a shy and embarrassed laugh like we'd both been caught with an orange rind covering our teeth.

"It's been a long time," I said.

"When was the last time we saw each other?" she asked, playing cool like she'd forgotten.

"The graduation party two years ago." My cheeks burned again. An image flickered into my mind of her summer-naked thigh pressed up closely against mine in the doorway between Holly Buford's kitchen and garage.

"Oh, yeah," Karen said, jutting her chin forward and lingering her eyes on mine for a moment and a half. "Well, come on in." She nodded her head back and stepped away from the door to let me in.

"Your folks here?" Jason poked his head around the corner of the living room wall.

"Nope."

"Mind if I roll one?" He headed over to the couch, taking up all three spaces as he spread his knees wide and leaned over the coffee table.

"Go ahead," she sighed—only slightly bored.

Jason leaned back, pulled a baggie from deep inside his pocket, leaned forward, and spread out his wares. "So how 'bout we go to Craig's?" He looked down, fiddling with the papers, portioning the weed.

"I don't think so." Karen sank into the crook of the loveseat's elbow, adjacent to the couch. I sat down next to her.

"Pffsssh," Jason let out an air noise. Craig was Jason's best friend since high school.

"Jason, you know I can't stand Craig." She rolled her eyes.

"You don't *usually* have a problem with it," Jason said.

"Yes, I do, Jason." Karen lowered her head but kept her eyes fixed on him. "We argue about it every time."

"Whatever." Jason squinted up his left eye but did not stop looking at his hands rolling the joint. "You comin'?" He asked me.

"So you're going?" Karen sounded annoyed but not surprised.

"I already called him and said I was coming over in half an hour." He raked the spilled green bits into a pile.

"When was that?" Karen asked. "Before you called me or after we made our plans?"

"Jesus Christ, I don't know. It was like 20 minutes ago, whenever that was." Jason licked the paper's edge, sealed the joint. "Come on, sis, Karen must be on the rag."

"Fuck you." Karen scrunched up her pretty face and bugged her eyes out. "She doesn't have to go with you to that asshole's house. I can take her home."

Jason poured the pile into the baggie, sealed it, and shoved everything back into his pocket. Then he looked at me and said, "What are you gonna do?"

"I'll stay here." I shrugged, trying to smooth the knot of parental-like struggle that hung over me.

"Whatever. Later." Jason sprang up from the couch and slammed the door behind him as he left.

"Ass-hole," Karen said flatly, enunciating each syllable. "Your brother's such an asshole, you know that?" She folded her arms and looked at me.

"Sometimes, yes." I sucked in a short breath and tightened my mouth. "So why are you with him?"

She shrugged one shoulder. "He can be nice sometimes." She paused, looking for a better reason. "And we get along when we're not fighting."

"When's that?"

Karen laughed. "Less and less often. It's pretty hot in here, huh?"

"I guess."

Karen turned away from me and took off her gray wool sweater, which was big and shapeless and probably Jason's. Jason's sweater, Jason's girlfriend. Her shoulder blades lifted with her arms, slid like giant butterfly wings or smallish elephant ears beneath her skin, under her thin white T-shirt. I noticed the architecture of her bones through the flimsy white cotton: the snake of her spine running from her swan neck connecting to the bridge of her ribs then to the dipped valley of her lower back and finishing off in an upward curve of a brushstroke.

"You know, I always hated you," Karen said.

"Thanks for being so candid."

"You know what I mean."

I arched an eyebrow, wrinkled my forehead. "I do?"

Karen drew her legs in and folded them under, like scissors or a map. "Envy. You were always so smart."

"Oh."

"I always wanted to be smart."

"Well," I said, "I always wanted to be devastatingly beautiful, so I guess we've both got something the other wants."

"Looks like." Karen's spidery eyes traveled from my mouth to my knees and scattered along the places in between, uprooting the solidity of my molecules.

"Wanna trade?" I twitched up my face because I couldn't bear the weight of the air hanging above the seat cushion between us.

She didn't say anything, just kept looking at me, so I said, "Tell me for real, why are you dating my brother?"

"Because I can't have his sister."

"Ha ha. Very Jerry Springer–like of you."

Karen put her hands on the cushion between us and leaned toward me. Her hair fell around the sides of her face. Her eyes locked onto mine for the second or third time that evening, and because they were more engaging than an eclipse, I couldn't look away. "Shit," I said. "You're Jason's girlfriend."

She made a small, squeaky *hmmmm* sound and said, "I'm my own person."

Since Karen was clearly factually beautiful, and Jason was gone...and since Karen looked as if she might be filled with apricot juice and was leaning so close to me that I could tell her shoulders were made of silk, not cheap satin, and might taste like vanilla ice cream with real vanilla beans, only warm...and since Karen's lips were so close that they were in danger of brushing mine anyway, I leaned my face in a little closer and we kissed.

I traced her bones with the tip of my finger and then with the tip of my tongue. I followed the way her shoulders sloped into her arms and bent at the elbow then ran from her forearms to her wrists and finally to her slender fingers. She fit neatly in the palms of my hands. Our curves met exactly where they should. And maybe everything wasn't perfect. We probably made sounds that we'd be embarrassed to hear in another context. We didn't discover the great love of our lives. I'm sure it probably won't happen again. And there were stumbles and giggles on both of our parts, neither knowing where this was going or why. But I did find out what Karen wanted to do with those small fingers and strong hands of hers. They were made for molding clay, not waiting tables or serving Jason greasy food and fuzzy liquid grains.

The next morning, Jason and I got up before sunrise, but not before Dad, who was already pacing in front of the TV, chewing and snorting and reeling off his "It doesn't look good. Snow, ice…"

Jason chain-smoked all the way from Winder to the highway, then finally asked, "You got that Beastie Boys tape?"

I pulled the tape out from the front pocket of my overalls.

"They fuckin' rock, don't you think?" Jason said.

"Yeah." It's a shame we can't really talk about much else. Safe topics: Dad, music, high school, Jason's job anecdotes.

After we were well into South Carolina, Jason said, "What's up? You haven't said much."

"Not much to say."

Jason shrugged. "We should have brought Karen with us. That'd be fun, huh?"

A finger of cold wormed its way up the back of my neck, sending icy shoots back down my spine and into my shoulder blades. I said nothing, looked out the window, tried to hum.

"What's wrong? Didn't you like her?"

"I liked her just fine." My cheeks were getting hotter.

"I thought y'all got along really well. What time did she bring you home last night? Past midnight, wasn't it?"

"Yeah."

"So what did y'all do?"

"Nothing."

"She's pretty hot, huh?"

So there I was, having to sit in Jason's car with his comment about Karen spilling into my ears and swishing around my head, trickling down my throat, and washing over my shoulders. As if my head was a toilet that'd been flushed, my brain traveling down the drain of my neck.

I could feel my back tense into that prim posture I get sometimes that causes Jason to call me a prude. I rolled up my eyes, suppressed a sigh, and looked out my side window.

"So what'd you think of her?"

I turned toward him and in a flat and steady tone said, "Remember how I'm a lesbian?"

He shrugged. "Yeah, that's why I asked. I wonder if we have the same taste."

"We do," I said. "I kissed her."

Jason said nothing. For several miles. I started thinking that either he didn't hear me, he didn't believe me, or I didn't really say it. When we crossed into North Carolina he asked, "So who kissed who first?"

"I don't know," I said. "I guess it was equal. I don't want to talk about this. It's making me uncomfortable."

"Oh, so it doesn't make you uncomfortable to mess around with my girlfriend, but it makes you uncomfortable to talk about it?" He shifted his tone from snide to sneery. "You don't get to decide what you want to talk about here." He pointed at me then patted his chest to punctuate his statement. "This is my car." Pat. "My girlfriend." Pat. "My conversation." Pat.

"Fuck you," I said quietly, muttering under my breath.

The car rapidly began to slow down. Jason swerved toward the shoulder of the road, pressing heavily on the brakes, tires squealing somewhat, car wanting to fishtail yet resisting. Luckily it wasn't snowing.

"Get out," Jason said. His teeth were stuck together like someone had locked his jaw but left his lips free to move, like a cheap ventriloquist.

He looked like he was in a movie—distant and fuzzy, flailing his arms and fuming, making a buzzing sound in my ears as the soundtrack blared out and the reel flapped in its wheel.

"Get the fuck out, I said." He turned toward me. This

movement jolted the movie forward into action again. The capillaries beneath the skin in his face began to expand, surface, heat up, like little radiators or stove coils.

I couldn't move.

Jason leaned over and pulled on the door handle. The door wouldn't open. "Goddamn it!" he spat. He jumped out of his side of the car, ran to my side, and grabbed the handle. Door was locked. "Fuck!" he pounded the roof of the car. He ran to his side of the car again, grabbed his keys out of the ignition, ran back around, and unlocked my door. "You're such a bitch," he told me, screaming it into my face in case I could have missed hearing him, and grabbed my arm. I released the seat belt clasp to escape getting choked. He pulled me out of the car and shoved me toward the grass.

Jason got back in the car, started up the engine with a forceful *vroom,* slammed his door, and squealed the tires as he drove off. As I watched the car move away, my backpack leapt from the window onto the side of the road.

I ran to pick it up. Then I could see that there was an exit up ahead with a gas station. My brother's taillights faded in the distance. The mountain air smelled fresh, crisp, non-smoky. The cars speeding past me on the highway caused a *whoosh* of wind to breeze past my hatless bald head. The fingers of cold brushed the back of my neck, kissed the tips of my ears.

And just then, as I was walking along the interstate in southern North Carolina, an ever-so-light, six-pointed crystalline flake floated from the sky, like a feather from a bird that had just been shot.

The Words I Know,
The Way I Understand

T. J. Bryan a.k.a. Tenacious

These are the words I know: *lesbian, queer, gay, vagina, cunnilingus, church, Wellesley, Pride Day,* and *IWD.* Words I have taken b(l)ack: *Wicca, buller, sodomite, poum-poum, poonani, pussy suckin', hurricane season, Crop Over, ackee (the Bajan kind), fishcake, extended* and *chosen family, Africa, Middle Passage* and *Barbados, home.* There are things I have woven into my life: eating pussy smelling strong of musk and cinnamon, making sweet bread and black cake on holidays, my right arm stiff and sore from wrestling with a full pot of *coo-coo,* the feel of the word *Bajan* as it rolls off my tongue, the sound of the name *Wicca* when she calls out to my soul.

I am coming out in/to realization of mySELF. I came out lacking knowledge. I was maybe all of 23 years old. There was more history in me than I allowed myself to see. There were more people holding up my insides than I could admit.

Touching, kissing, fucking her, I was gathered up into the arms of our mothers. We licked and finger-fucked, comin' ecstatically into a no-man's land of unspoken desires. I found the spot, the wet fertile place between our clits, our culture, and our past. I came home for the first time.

Her fingers filled me up. Filled me with lost pieces of my past. I remember....

The first night we lay in bed, where I had placed myself hoping she would fuck my brains out. For six hours we talked, giggled, and shared, not touching, on extreme opposite sides of her futon. Two Black Bajan Wiccas choking on our shyness, unable to cross the chasm between need and passion realized.

Me: "You know my Uncle Jean the barber?"

Her: "Your father is Jean's brother? He used to cut my father's hair years ago. Everybody knows Jean."

Me: "I don't. I remember him from the last time I went to Barbados. I have a picture of him, though."

This was a beginning for us, but especially for me. I was becoming....

She doesn't make me fried flying fish with enough pepper to make my eyes run water anymore. When you're both striving to be the other person's mother-lover-sister-healer-protector, the closeness becomes too much.

I still crave the sight and sound of my sistren gathered in love and struggle though. In my mind's eye, there's a place where we're all talkin' at once. There's life-saving variety here. Differences of fashion, food, taste, and sexual practice are honored, not reviled. We get more excited. Our eyes brighten. And the laughter? Our laughter combined breaks all sound barriers and does a two-step on top of our pain and the funky chicken on our internalized hatred of ourselves. Our words become a sweet cacophony of creative self-expression. In the fiery glare of our emerging spirits we are continually burnt to a crisp and remade with hope. We are West Indian lesbians of African descent, and when we come home, culture, joy, and pain seep out through our pores like sweat.

Around them and sometimes in my writing I use my own hybrid chat—a shaky mixture of Barbadian, Jamaican patois learned from the kids I grew up with, urban Black folk talk, and whiter-than-white Canadian speak. One of them says I'm looking *maga* and asks if I'm losing weight. A chorus of sucked teeth speaks volumes about our love of big wimmin, round hips, soft, yielding flesh, and high, fat butts. This is something I came to appreciate, but not before my socialized love of scrawny bodies cost me the trust of my first love.

They cradle me in a familiar intensity of emotion. Understanding my words and the untongued spaces too. There's loudness and exuberance here but none of the accusations I often hear from wimmin of color or in white spaces about violent, Black, West Indian wimmin who are too rude, intimidating, and unsubtle to be tolerated. I don't have to hold back. I can breathe deeply, taking in the smell of sweaty armpits, just-fucked pussy, and freshly oiled hair. I hold tight onto flesh and feel strong forearms wrapped round me. Their soft, thick lips brush my cheeks in greeting. I'm alive as I can only be with them.

I fear this. Or more correctly, I fear the temporariness of it. Fear the times when we are together because this inevitably leads me to the times when we are not. Forces me to acknowledge the fact of being on my own, without someone to guard my back when I stand trembling with just the memory of our togetherness to get me through the night. I live a half-life where I feel unwhole, only half a woman, part queer, only a little Caribbean and slightly African, when I am not with them.

The courage of vulnerability is needed for me to form links with them and our herstory. Away from the context they provide, thoughts are hard to form and my mouth has trouble shaping the words we usually share. I feel that loss every time we say goodbye, every time a relationship or friendship ends.

Taking my place among them is about opening up. About letting them flow deep inside me, allowing them to stroke and savor the places where my soul is stored. Long-buried, precious memories of my grandmother's house in Barbados rise from that place. So many wimmin—my grandmother, mother, sister, aunts, and others—taught me most of what I know. Not since the age of 8, since I left Barbados, left all that behind, have I felt so understood and so exposed.

So often I find myself searching for insubstantial glimmerings of wimmin from my past in the curves of Black lesbians I know now. This one has my sister's big, sad eyes. That one standing tall reminds me of my aunts in their youth. Tears of remembrance and the shrill laughter of childhood mingle and cavort near the surface of my will.

I fear and admire the ways the adult and the child in me are reflected in their gaze. Am I home yet? Can I rest now? I need to. But I struggle with this unfamiliar intimacy. It's been so long. And I don't want to get accustomed to something that may not be in my life tomorrow. I've mourned the loss of family forever. Whether I'm talking about chosen, extended, or biological family, grief and loneliness are never far away.

My sisters' clear-eyed view of my dark-skinned self scrapes uncomfortably at the armor I wear. Sovereign boundaries are crossed too often for comfort. The cyclic ebb and flow of our lives—together then apart, together, apart, feels too much like abandonment. And I'm not brave enough to risk that again. The cynic in me can't open herself to love unquestioningly anymore. Instead I seek the consistency and stability of solitude. Caught up in the grip of self-imposed isolation, I wonder, will I continue to remember who I am? Who will comb my hair and massage out muscles knotted tight with unexpressed emotion? Who will speak my true name and bury me when I am dead?

Small-Town Girl Makes Dyke

Sally Miller Gearhart

Miss Zella Woodrum (Miss Zudie) and Miss Maude Caroline Pucket Miller swung back and forth in their rockers in front of Miss Zudie's fire. "I declare, Miss Zudie," said Maude Caroline in a low voice (convinced that since I was in the bathroom, I would not hear her), "the day Frank Miller died was the day my life began!"

"Is that so!" Miss Zudie reached across the hassock that sat between them and touched my grandmother's arm. "Well, Miss Maude, they all say that life begins at 40!"

My grandmother responded with words I could not distinguish, and the two women collapsed into rolls of laughter, rocking and nodding and embellishing the conversation with further low-spoken comments.

We were in the midst of our weekly visit to Miss Zudie's (to be paralleled in three days' time by her weekly visit to our house), precious pastime, sacred rituals. The only thing that could have threatened these intensely anticipated occasions might have been a spontaneous bridge game, for in the '30s, Pearisburg (pronounced "Parisburg") citizens lived each day fixated on bingo, radio, or bridge. But Miss Maudie had very deliberately disciplined herself on this matter: She played bridge regularly two nights a week and at the drop of a hat, *except* on the evenings that she and Miss Zudie were to get together. Nothing, not even the eventual advent of duplicate bridge in our town, ever kept Maude Miller away from her visits with Miss Zella Woodrum.

I liked it best when we were the visitors. Maudie would bundle me up in my leggings—or if it was summer she'd hand me my sweater—grab her knitting, and up the street we'd go to the rambling old gray house on the corner. Maybe we'd sit in front of Miss Zudie's stove in the kitchen, where the walls were papered with calendars in exact order back to 1887 and where hundreds of small and large empty matchboxes were neatly stacked on every available shelf surface or windowsill. Miss Zudie never threw anything away. Usually she meticulously wrapped it and gave it a label. Once, in my explorations of the old house, I discovered a small box marked STRINGS TOO SHORT TO USE. Inside were strings. Too short to use.

Or maybe the two women would sit in front of the fireplace in Miss Zudie's cozy bedroom. I was the needle-threader and, when there was yarn to be rolled up, official skein-holder. Miss Zudie always saw to the tea or coffee or warm cider, and Maudie would make a big ceremony out of cutting yarn or thread with the penknife she carried forever in her pocketbook, a gift to her from me and Miss Zudie. "Comes in so handy for so many things!" she'd exclaim. "The other day I used it to cut back that forsythia bush."

In warm weather the two women sat in wicker chairs under the big maples in Miss Zudie's weed-high yard. They swatted at gnats and sipped lemonade and meandered from subject to subject and back again. I remember most vividly their absorption with genealogy—what was the name of Yance Peter's second boy, who had married the Woolwine girl from Clover Hollow and did that or did that not make Ola Brotherton and Bess Pasterfield second cousins once-removed? And with propriety—how Miss Maudie's relatives out on Curve Road still butchered the King's English, saying "hadda went," "coulda took," "ought to have saw," and "like to have fell."

Whatever the season, wherever they were, and whatever those two talked about, I loved to lean against Maudie's legs and just let their voices roll over me. Vocal caresses, intimate and warm, always punctuated by the formal "Miss Zudie" and "Miss Maude."

Sometimes one of them would say, "Why don't you go on out and talk to Mr. Bill?" Reluctantly I'd relocate to the front porch, where Miss Zudie's brother watched the town go by from his high perch above the street. Mr. Bill, like Miss Zudie, had never married, but unlike her he rarely socialized. He could lay a splash of tobacco juice right between your toes with the accuracy of a sharpshooter, and he carved wonderful ornate bedposts from cherry wood. I figured he had things to teach me.

Just after her death nearly 40 years later, I found among my grandmother's things a faintly scented packet of letters from Miss Zudie, written when she made her yearly visit down to Clintwood. In one of them she had written, "Oh, how I long to get home again and to hear you coming up the path to my kitchen door. The sound of your footsteps sets my heart to pounding!"

Until I came along, Maude Miller was the only woman of the Puckett-Miller clan to "get educated." She'd earned a teaching degree in 1901 at Martha Washington, a women's college. The temper of her steel was truly tested in 1929, when my grandfather died and the Great Depression descended on our Appalachian town. Maudie didn't drop a stitch. She turned down four would-be husbands that I was aware of (and probably more), converted our home into a rooming house, took up teaching high school (yearly salary: $100), and embarked on a life that ultimately earned her the reputation of a town character.

She fired her own furnace, rebuilt her own kitchen, remained the only Republican in a fiercely Democratic family, got "churched" for playing bridge on Sunday, and mowed her own grass (once, I remember, at midnight, while I held the flashlight and she recited "The Charge of the Light Brigade"). She learned to drive at 65 and, characteristically, drove in the middle of the street, trusting that any policeman who apprehended her—or any judge who tried her case—would be either one of her past students or blood kin, neither of whom would do more than reprimand Miz Miller/Aunt Maude.

I went back to Pearisburg in 1974 to see my family. When Maudie heard me drive up, she leapt out of her chair with excitement, for we hadn't seen each other in four years. In that moment, she fell and broke her hip, a condition to which her active spirit was never reconciled. She died alone in a nursing home within a year.

It is not true, as the folks in town say, that she died in triumph playing a seven-no-trump hand. But it is true that there were two things on her bedside table: an old penknife and a deck of cards.

* * *

When my mother (Maudie's daughter) was a child, she and her best friend were inseparable. In the warm summers when nightfall overtook them in their play, my mother, Sarah Elizabeth, called "Dit," would protectively walk Phoebe home over the four blocks between their houses. Then Phoebe would walk Dit home so she wouldn't be scared. And, of course, Dit would have to walk Phoebe home again. I picture them giggling and holding hands, swinging up and down the maple-lined streets of Pearisburg, far into the magic evenings.

They were once in a play together where one of them (they could never remember which one) was named "Miss Laurie." For the rest of their lives, through marriages, children, separations, depression, death, family scandals, and genteel poverty, the two women called each other "Miss Laurie," still visiting regularly, still exchanging birthday and Christmas gifts, still talking long hours on the phone. My mother's death ended their 70-year friendship, and until she herself died, Miss Phoebe placed flowers on Miss Dit's grave every August 10, her birthday.

The Crash of 1929 had catapulted Miss Dit out of her only year in college and into the arms of my handsome, drinking, gambling, womanizing, reprobate father. Her divorce from him when I was two was unheard of, because once married, the women of Pearisburg stayed that way, often simply enduring a grim fate. It was the first divorce of the county's history. With no skills and a child to support, Dit moved to Richmond, 250 miles away, to learn typing and shorthand at night while she worked by day as a stenographer in the Home Owners' Loan Corporation, one of FDR's antidotes to the failed national economy.

I lived with her in Richmond until I was school-age, cared for by Katherine Summers, the black woman who had escaped Pearisburg with Dit and who ultimately found work and love and a family in Richmond. The boarding house at three-oh-two West Franklin Street (an address I was drilled on lest I become lost in the city) was run by Mrs. Hardaway and her daughter. It was peopled by single or divorced women, who, like my mother, had come from all over the state to find jobs. Dit and I shared a bedroom with two other women, warm happy souls who played cards and dominos with me.

I loved my times with Katherine, spent mostly in the kitchen with Susie, the cook, or out in Monroe Park's sandbox—where Chucky Klotz once called me a sissy for having a doll. That resulted in my first full-fledged fight, one I have always believed I won, though Katherine (whom I still visit in Richmond even after these 50-odd years) has a different notion of that encounter.

Fun though the park was, I always looked forward to 6 o'clock, when most of the women came home to strip off their uniforms or wiggle out of their corsets and hose and tight shoes. I would sit on the stairs between the second and third floors and listen to them sighing with relief and calling out to one another the excitements of the day, the contentments of at last being home. I remember dinnertime as a loud affair, full of boisterous conversation and laughter, tales of woe, and teasings about boyfriends—who never, somehow, materialized on the premises.

Three-oh-two was a house of women. Even after her return to Pearisburg many years later, my mother kept up correspondence and visits with her friends there, and she told me just before she died that those years in Richmond in that boardinghouse, those hard times of the Great Depression, had actually been the freest and happiest in her adult life.

* * *

After I started school back in Pearisburg, I could only visit my mother, my Katherine, and my Richmond boardinghouse during summertime, when Maudie would take me on the Norfolk and Western's Powhatan Arrow from Ripplemead down through the low mountain passes and winding rivers to the flatlands of eastern Virginia. In other seasons I was exploring caves or mountaintops with the 4-H Club, playing kick the can in the fresh spring nights, swinging from grapevines, falling from trees, casting down long white winter hills, or (with the girls) defending snow or stickweed forts against "the boys," on whom we had early on declared war and with whom we seemed constantly to be in physical fights that cost us our lunch hours and our recesses.

The companion of many of my days was Wanza, five years my senior, and so "high yeller" that we were often mistaken for sisters. Wanza's job for the six years we were together was to keep me out of trouble while Maudie conducted her affairs of school and rooming house. Wanza taught me to cux, wrassle, box, play mumblety-peg, put English on my steelies so I could be a marbles champion, and sail a stickweed straight and far. Best of all, when we went to the movies I'd get to sit with her in the balcony with the black folks, where the most fun always was and where the best commentary on the film always took place.

And Wanza taught me to run, coaching me on how to conserve my breath—how to breathe solely through my nose at first and then, after the big exhaustion came, how to capture the miracle of the second wind. Wanza ran everywhere—to work, to school, to the grocery store, to the sinkhole, up and down the big hill to Bluff City—and when she was 16, she ran straight to the big heart and ample arms of Bob Bleddins, one of the town's derelicts, whom Wanza's mama was for some reason ashamed for her to associate with. I only later realized Wanza was shacking up with him.

So we sometimes hung out with Bob, always on the sly and with me sworn not to tell Wanza's mama. Though he taught me some of the subtleties of crapshooting, I remember sometimes being jealous of Wanza's attentions to this man. More than 25 years later, when I was taking her to Roanoke for her operation for throat cancer, I confessed that jealousy to her. "Pshaw!" Wanza sputtered. "That man meant shit to me, don't you know that? Just company, that's all." Then she fixed me with those soft brown eyes. "It was you and me, that's who," she said. "You and me, to kingdom come. Right?"

Wanza died the following year. I wasn't there to see her ushered into heaven, but I'm sure she went in running.

* * *

The text of my childhood was the patriarchal one: men are the more important sex; they have the information, the skills, the tools, the opportunities, and the say-so; women participate in knowledge and power only through men. That text was articulated for me by movies, schools, churches, newspapers, books, magazines, and radio programs; certainly I saw it at work in the social structures of my small town and in the big city of Richmond.

Yet the unspoken message of my days, the subtext of my childhood, was a different one: *Men do not matter.* No voice spoke those words, no headline announced it, no sermon suggested it. The women who surrounded me simply lived their lives as if men were, though occasionally nice or some-times interesting, basically insignificant. Women, they seemed to say, are the source of power, the heart of action, the focal point of love. Women trust, honor, and enjoy one another.

That subtext became a fundamental part of my world-view, sustaining me in rough times and firing in me a tremen-dous creative energy; more recently it has granted me hope that the earth can be restored, that all its creatures can regain their sanity, health, freedom, and dignity.

Though most of the women of Pearisburg and those of the Richmond boardinghouse would be offended to be called les-bians, in my experience they differ from lesbians only in their lack of sexual experience with other women. Granted, that's a *significant* lack, but it is not a *signifying* lack. Certainly sexu-al love with another woman can transform the quality of a woman's every subsequent behavior or attitude. But other acts between women may be equally transformative. We all know women who call themselves lesbians but who have not yet had a sexual experience with another woman. We also know women who have had sexual experiences with other women who identify as heterosexual. I've decided that though sex has enhanced my lesbianism and empowered my womanness, it hasn't in itself made me a lesbian.

Still, the words *lesbian* or *gay* or *homosexual* and the myths and stereotypes that attended these words struck fear into the hearts of the women of my hometown. When I told my mother I was a lesbian, her response was "Can you get an operation?" When I told my grandmother, she became "sick to the ends of my toes," because I was something "unnatural." Katherine Summers, a pillar of the African Methodist Episcopal Zion Church, said, after a long silence, "I love you anyway." Miss Phoebe's daughter changed the subject. Wanza was the sole exception of the experience: She grinned and said, "No shit." Even after the advent of the women's movement, even now in these days of open discussion and debate, the words are highly charged.

I've often asked myself over these past two decades why families, friends, coworkers, acquaintances, even strangers still have such trouble handling our coming out as lesbians. Certainly our saying who we are identifies the previously ignored hippopotamus in the living room and forces those we tell to deal with our "sin" or "sickness." And certainly by coming out we offend any narrow view of sexuality or rigid religious dogma. Politically, of course, our coming out threatens patriarchy and the nuclear family—we aren't behaving like regular girls, fussing over men, marrying them, having *their* babies.

I am convinced, though, that the women I grew up with had (or would have had) such an extreme and negative reaction to my coming out not because they thought I was damned or evil or sick or flying in the face of God's laws. They froze and trembled and cried and said, "Sh-h-h-h!" because my coming out was too close to home, because their own lives were testimonies to precisely the "abomination" I was proudly claiming for myself. Perhaps by announcing it so loudly, by trying to make their subtext into a text, I threatened the security of their world in a way they did not consciously recognize.

In 1972 I went to New York to be on Tom Snyder's *Tomorrow* show, where three other women and I discussed our pride and joy at being lesbians. Pearisburg, Va., of course, had its late-night viewers, and by noon the following day (I'm told by still-closeted sources there), the news was all over town that Sally Miller Gearhart was on national television "being homosexual." All over town, that is, except to the ears of my mother and grandmother. It's a testimony, I guess, to what they would consider their good taste or their respect for my family that even good friends of my folks never told them of my appearance on that show. In fact, I had already come out to my mother and grandmother. So there was the town protecting my family from what it thought they didn't know, and there was my family, knowing the dark secret but not knowing that everyone else knew.

I like to think that in some part of themselves the women in my hometown who heard about or saw that show—Wanza, Miss Zudie, Miss Phoebe and her daughter, my old piano teacher, my old English teacher, three or four nurses at the hospital, a lot of the girls I went to school with, my mother's coworkers, some of my grandmother's bridge partners—knew that my joy and pride in loving other women was at least in part a legacy from them and from the women of my family, that what I was saying to them was a simple "Thank you." I like to think that they then nodded to me an equally simple "You're welcome."

Dream-Catcher

Ellen S. Jaffe

I've heard what you hate
about coming to workshop
is sleeping alone
nightmares that come in the dark
in a narrow bed
perhaps this isn't true, but if it is
I'd like to sleep with you there
hold you against the dark
it wouldn't matter about lovers
in other places, gay or straight,
or even about sex, though I've wondered
about your hand touching me *there, there...*
it's a matter of cold and warm
terror of slippery things
stuck where they don't belong
melting in the mist that rises
from our skin
as we dream each other's dreams.

I offer you a temporary nest
in the room of my own
where I give birth,
rescue wounded cougars,
see White Buffalo Woman,
while I take, for tonight,
whatever demons lurk under the bridge
of your mind
and send them packing with my magic words.

But probably I'll say nothing.
Maybe I don't want to embarrass you, maybe
I'm afraid of being hurt,
unused now to loving women
(unused to loving).
The best I can give is watchfulness,
a look, a cautious touch, a word
about our poems,
the lack of desire of daisies
quietly growing
and the cat who stares at them
not stalking but dreaming.

We hug goodbye, touch cheeks cool as petals,
and wave again at the stoplight.
I turn north to the highway,
you drive along the lakeshore, heading home.
I hope tonight
you have sweet dreams.